PRAISE FOR *MAN ENOUGH*

Man Enough is a fearless and faithful clarion call for the children of God to conform to the image of Jesus Christ, not to cultural or religious stereotypes around masculinity. With his trademark wisdom and humility, Nate Pyle assesses harmful misconceptions about what it means to be a man, shares his own story and the stories of others who don't necessarily fit the mold, and returns to Scripture to forge a better way forward—a way of freedom, truth, and grace. This book is a must-read, one I'll be recommending to friends and readers for years to come. Every page is an invitation to liberation.

Rachel Held Evans, author of *Searching for Sunday* and *A Year of Biblical Womanhood*

"Blessed are the tough, muscled, and masculine." Jesus never said anything remotely like this, but some modern believers act as if he did. Some Christians have transformed Jesus into John Wayne to promote culturally driven ideas about what it means to be a man. Thankfully, Nate Pyle dismantles false notions of manhood and replaces them with a more biblical concept of being human. If you read only one book on biblical manhood, it should be this one!

Jonathan Merritt, author of *Jesus Is Better Than You Imagined* and senior columnist for Religion News Service

This book sets men free from the culture-driven standards of masculinity and welcomes us into a Jesus-shaped humanity. Going beyond the tired old stereotypes of manhood, Nate Pyle gives us a redeemed vision for what it means to be a man after God's own heart. Deeply pastoral, well-written, and insightful, this book will bring healing to many.

Sarah Bessey, author of *Jesus Feminist*

Wow! Nate Pyle has written a brilliant and much-needed book. He has exposed all of our culturally driven views of manhood that conflict with who Jesus calls men to be. The self-made, independent, muscle-bound, don't-take-nothing-from-no-one American man shares little in common with Jesus as he's revealed in Scripture. Thank you, Nate, for writing this book! Now I don't have to.

Preston Sprinkle, PhD, vice president for Eternity Bible College's Boise extension and author of *Charis: God's Scandalous Grace for Us* and *Fight: A Christian Case for Nonviolence*

Nate Pyle's *Man Enough* offers a surprisingly unique take on the topic of biblical masculinity. By centering the conversation on the ideals of Jesus, Pyle not only challenges many of the stereotypical concepts regarding evangelical masculinity but also offers a broader and more varied perspective for what it means to be a man in light of the gospel. His delivery is gracious and thoughtful, tackling "manhood" without ego and arrogance. Through a pastoral lens—using both theology and self-deprecation to his favor— Pyle expounds deeply on what it means to be both Christian and man.

Matthew Paul Turner, author of *Churched*
and *Our Great Big American God*

In a world where many of us wrestle with chronic feelings of inadequacy and engage in a constant state of comparing ourselves to both others and invented ideals, Nate Pyle's *Man Enough* speaks much-needed words of healing and validation. With the heart of a pastor and the pen of a poet, Nate invites us to reconsider the source of our cultural concepts of masculinity and helps us to rediscover a manhood beyond some of the not-so-helpful messages we've received over the years. This book is one I found to be soothing ointment on old wounds—a message I wish I'd been given before I transitioned into adulthood but am tremendously grateful to have now. Rarely does a first-time author hit it out of the park on their first swing, but that's exactly what Nate has done. *Man Enough* is one of those books that deserves to be moved to the top of the pile.

Benjamin L. Corey, author of *Undiluted:
Rediscovering the Radical Message of Jesus*

When we talk about "being a man" in Christian circles, the conversation often centers around a distorted image of masculinity that doesn't represent the life, ministry, and calling of Christ. To put it bluntly, the church needs a bigger dose of Jesus in its dialogue about manhood. Thank goodness we can count on Nate Pyle for that. In *Man Enough*, we're finally offered a refreshing perspective on male identity—one that is centered fully on the depth of Christ rather than on the one-dimensional, cage-fighting model of our culture. As a woman married to a man and a mother to a son, I'm so grateful for Nate's brave writing and leadership in these pages. This is a must-read for both women and men in the church, and I can't recommend it enough.

Nish Weiseth, author of *Speak: How
Your Story Can Change the World*

Man Enough breaks from the pack of man-books to liberate men from false conceptions of masculinity. Male readers will not come away with a deflated sense that they are never man enough. Women readers will encounter a brand of manhood here that gives hope to the men they love. Nate Pyle's search for answers recaptures a gospel vision of manhood that is good news for both men and women.

Carolyn Custis James, author of *Malestrom: Manhood Swept into the Currents of a Changing World*

Nate Pyle has brought charitable and generous consideration to a topic marked by hostility and resentment. A fine work of biblical meditation, cultural critique, and prayerful study, *Man Enough* challenges conservative and liberal notions of gender norms while encouraging meaningful dialogue between the two. In a pastoral and convicting manner, Pyle has authored a book well-suited to the needs of our time.

Preston Yancey, canon theologian and author of *Tables in the Wilderness: A Memoir of God Found, Lost, and Found Again*

Nate Pyle's book is a timely contribution to a sadly one-sided conversation on masculinity. Through an engagement with Scripture, sociology, and honest self-disclosure, Nate invites us to conform not to some contemporary "muscular" version of masculinity but to the vulnerable Lamb, in whom we need not strive, perform, or prove ourselves. His chapter on Jesus is worth the price of the book alone. I pray that *Man Enough* is used as a pathway to freedom and vulnerability for men.

Dr. Chuck DeGroat, associate professor of pastoral care at Western Theological Seminary and author of *The Toughest People to Love*

The Spirit of the Lord brings freedom, and I can sense the Spirit of the Lord all over the pages of this book. Men will find freedom from their insecurities, the standards of others, and the combative manliness that has taken hold in some Christian circles. Nate Pyle leads the way toward Christ-centered manhood with vulnerability, gentleness, and a sharp focus on the example of Jesus.

Ed Cyzewski, author of *A Christian Survival Guide* and *Coffeehouse Theology*

Vulnerable. Honest. Humble. Not words one usually associates with a book on manhood, but Nate Pyle nails them here. I love how *Man Enough* points us to Jesus and insists that our thinking must ultimately be centered around him. While Nate and I don't land in all the same places, I was refreshed by his boldness in declaring we must allow Christ to critique our cultural assumptions around what it means to be "man enough," because he is the One who is more than enough and the One who frees us from our posturing and pretending to become more truly human.

Joshua Ryan Butler, author of *The Skeletons in God's Closet*

Nate Pyle's heartfelt exploration of Jesus-shaped masculinity is both a confrontation and an invitation. It exposes all the places I attempt to hide, but it also beckons me to come out of hiding by choosing the road of risky vulnerability. I have nothing but high praise for *Man Enough.*

Steve Wiens, author of *Beginnings* (January 2016) and senior pastor of Genesis Covenant Church in Minneapolis, Minnesota

In our sexualized society where confusion reigns, Nate Pyle has written a much-needed book. Through powerful, vulnerable storytelling of his own journey into manhood, he offers a solidly biblical look at the journey that every man must take. He draws illustrations from academia and popular culture in a book that is both profound and easily readable. I highly recommend *Man Enough.*

Jim Herrington, founding director of Mission Houston

MAN
ENOUGH

MAN ENOUGH

HOW JESUS REDEFINES MANHOOD

NATE PYLE

ZONDERVAN

Man Enough
Copyright © 2015 by Nathan Pyle

This title is also available as a Zondervan ebook. Visit www.zondervan.com/ebooks.

Requests for information should be addressed to:
Zondervan, 3900 *Sparks Dr. SE, Grand Rapids, Michigan 49546*

Library of Congress Cataloging-in-Publication Data

Pyle, Nate.
     Man enough : how Jesus redefines manhood / Nate Pyle.—1st [edition].
       pages cm
     Includes bibliographical references.
     ISBN 978-0-310-34337-0 (softcover)
      1. Men (Christian theology) 2. Masculinity–Religious aspects–Christianity.
     I. Title.
     BT703.5.P95   2015
     248.8'42–dc23   2015016151

Published in association with literary agent Jenni Burke of D.C. Jacobson & Associates LLC, an Author Management Company www.dcjacobson.com

Cover design: Dual Identity
Cover photo: © Janka Dharmasena / iStockphoto®
Interior design: Kait Lamphere

First printing July 2015 / Printed in the United States of America

For Luke—
You have nothing to prove.

For Dad—
"The glory of children is their fathers."
Proverbs 17:6 ESV

CONTENTS

CHAPTER 1

OUT OF THE WILDERNESS

"Blessed are the meek,
for they will inherit the earth."

Matthew 5:5

I didn't feel like a man until I was thirty-one.

That sounds like an odd thing to say, even by today's standards, when adolescence extends well beyond the teenage years. You would think by the age of thirty-one the struggle to feel like a man would be long over. But it wasn't. Life moved forward without ever giving me that defining moment when I could say, "Now I am a man." Days added on to weeks that added on to months that added on to years, and now I was thirty-one. Which, when you say it out loud, is an age when you should feel like a man.

By all accounts, I had every reason to be secure in my manhood. I graduated from college, paid for my own car insurance, got married to a beautiful woman, got a job, bought a house, completed my master's degree, became a lead pastor, and had a child. Mission manhood complete. If there was ever a checklist to determine whether one was a man, my accomplishments should have earned a check in every box, and yet deep down, I felt like I still had to do something or prove something to show I was a man.

It felt like I was stuck in this no-man's land where I wasn't a teen or a college student, but I wasn't truly an adult yet. As a young pastor, I would lead meetings at church and feel like the kid who got invited to sit at the grown-ups' table for Thanksgiving. I constantly felt the need to apologize for my age during sermons or counseling sessions—as if my age disqualified me from speaking and having an opinion. I had long ago memorized the verse where Paul exhorts Timothy not to "let anyone look down on you because you are young,"[1] but that didn't make me feel like a man. It just reminded me that, despite the fact I could be a pastor at the ripe old age of twenty-eight, with all the right qualifications, people would still look down on me, and I would have to prove I was capable.

So in the midst of all of this, it felt like something else needed to happen to validate crossing the boy-to-man threshold. Some event, some feeling, some experience, some *thing* was needed to help me feel like a man.

I eventually got that experience. But in no way was it what I expected would make me feel like a man.

In the fall of 2010, I went to Houston for a leadership retreat with my denomination. I had been involved with this particular leadership initiative for the past two years, and this retreat was a kickoff for the next two years of the initiative.

The weekend started out horribly. Ten minutes before the retreat began, I got a call from my bank telling me there was fraudulent activity on one of our accounts. This forced me to excuse myself from most of the beginning sessions so I could ensure that our accounts were secure. On top of that, my wife was home with our eight-month-old son, who was, of course, being difficult — which always makes being away from home tough. Before I even participated in the retreat, I was mentally and emotionally exhausted.

Which was probably a good thing. It saved me from doing what I always do in situations where I want to look good: play the part of a man. I might not have felt like a man, but that didn't stop me from acting how I thought a man should act. I should have been nominated for an Oscar based on how well I played the confidently cool, good-looking guy with the answers but who was aloof enough to not care if you knew. Except I did care.

A lot.

For thirty years, I had perfected the art of looking good — and not just physically. Growing up in the church had taught me, not just the right answers to theological questions, but how to be authentic without being vulnerable. Being bullied about my weight in middle school trained me to look good physically. My competitive nature drives me to be the best, or at least not the worst. This resulted in a pretty attractive package on the outside. I can honestly say that people liked me. But all the effort to look good and craft an image I wanted people to see had an unintended consequence.

They liked the image, but they didn't know me.

But this time, I couldn't play the part. With everything happening back home, I was so emotionally drained that I didn't have the energy to pretend. Over the course of the weekend, that gnawing sense of loneliness began to creep from the back of my head to the front and settle into my consciousness. During the scheduled solitude times throughout the weekend, I began to clearly see that I was unknown. Not just by those at the retreat, but I was unknown in most of my relationships in life.

I didn't share this with my retreat small group because, frankly, I didn't know how to. Thirty years of practicing pretense meant that sharing what I truly felt scared the hell out of me. It would be death by exposure. I wasn't ready for that. Nor was I ready to share something that would be a blemish on the image I had spent thirty years perfecting.

The last session of the retreat was a prayer time. It was a time to share with one of the retreat leaders what God had revealed to each of us over the weekend and get prayer. You probably know what is going to happen here, and you're right. I went up for prayer. I stood in front of Jim—who has now become a dear friend and mentor. He put his hand on my shoulder, looked me in the eye, and softly smiled.

"What's going on?"

And then it began to slowly come out.

"I feel lonely."

"Why?"

"Because I don't feel like anyone really knows me."

"Why?" (I've learned my four-year-old can be a spiritual director, considering the fact that he asks the same question so often.)

"I don't let anyone get too close. I feel like if they really get to see me, then they will reject me. If they see all of me, then they will see I'm not good enough."

"Where else does this show up in your life?" he asked.

The question caught me off guard. *Where else does this show up?* My mind scrambled because if I didn't come up with a decent answer, I would look horrible. Heaven forbid that I look bad telling someone how I feel like crap.

At that point, I had a decision to make: do what I normally do and find a way to save face and come out looking good, or be honest. Maybe it was because I was tired, but for some unknown reason, I chose to be honest.

That decision has changed my life.

In that moment of honesty, the answer to Jim's question came almost immediately, but it surprised me. For crying out loud, I was a pastor. It couldn't be true. But it was.

"With God. I don't let him close because I think he will reject me."

It was an extremely emotional few moments for me. I talked about how it felt to acknowledge that God felt distant. I became present to how frightening it was to functionally believe that God could unconditionally love everyone, but that he would probably reject me. And Jim did everything right. He listened. He empathized. And then he told me that in two years of knowing me, this was the first time he felt like he could be near me. Jim affirmed the reality I have since discovered more fully. I had let my guard down, and in that moment, he came near and told me that now, in my vulnerability, I was approachable. Knowable. Lovable.

My efforts at projecting the perfect image made me unapproachable to him and others because the image was too perfect. Too good.

I began to see myself—myself in relationship to others, and myself in relationship to God—in a way I had never seen before. I began to see just how inauthentic I was, and how that inauthenticity was walling me off from being known.

This was a pivotal moment for me. Seeing myself and my actions clearly began a transformation in me that is still happening. The change didn't happen overnight, but slowly, and with intentional effort, I began to live with both authenticity and vulnerability. I stopped trying to be the perfect person, and I started trying to be me.

What's more, in that moment, the one when I was vulnerable and cried and shared my heart, I began feeling like a man.

The Beginning of a Transformation

Both Christian and non-Christian authors have couched masculinity in more primal terms. For example, Christian counselor John Eldredge's *Wild at Heart* and Harvard professor Robert Bly's *Iron John* both lament the growing number of feminized "nice guys" needing permission to recover their inner wildness and once again take forceful action in the world. And certainly, men should embrace and even celebrate their masculinity. But talking about gender raises a number of questions. What does it mean to be a man? Are there distinctives between men and women outside of anatomy? What do we do with the various expressions of masculinity that can exist between two men?

All throughout high school, I played soccer in a football town. Although we soccer players were athletes, we were considered field fairies compared to those who played a sport requiring more than small pieces of plastic stuffed in the front of their socks for protection. By and large, American culture treats soccer players the same way my high school locker room did—as less than men. Our current definition of masculinity doesn't make room for both soccer players and football players to be seen as men. Despite David Beckham's athletic success, wealth, and sex appeal, I've never seen him referred to as a "man's man." This overly simple example reveals the existence in our culture of one masculinity all men are told to strive for. Often, this masculinity sets the bar so dangerously high that, as *New York Times* columnist Charles Blow said in an interview, it is "writing a note to a song so high only a few people are meant to hit it, and nobody is meant to hold it."[2]

When we define masculinity by one's wildness, we choose a wildly narrow definition. Much of the work that has been done to define masculinity seeks to fit all men into the same rigid mold: wild, tough warriors who cannot be tamed. But what about the poet? What about the scholar? What about the man who would rather paint than wrestle? What about the man who would rather garden than fight? Are they not men?

Of course they are.

So let's change how we talk about being a man. Let's consider the possibility that there isn't a masculinity, but masculinities.

Men Do Manly Things?

I grew up across the street from a swamp. Not just a small bog, but a legitimate, Michigan woods swamp. If you walked out our front door and across the lawn, you would walk down a hill directly into the woods. After about seventy-five yards, the woods would begin to get swampy. Water, old trees fallen and moss covered, with young saplings growing up in their place—this was my wilderness. If you walked straight north for about two hundred yards, you would come to a large creek, Pigeon Creek. Theoretically, you could canoe down this creek to Lake Michigan, but because of the logs and fallen trees, it would be nearly impossible.

When I first started deer hunting, these were the woods I hunted.

I remember going out at twelve years old and scouting the land, trying to find that perfect hunting spot to place my tree stand—not just any tree stand, but my first. Even though it was so close to our house I could hear my parents talk when they were outside, it was, in my mind, still wilderness. The memory of the first time I hunted out of that stand—putting on my camouflage, grabbing my bow, and walking out into the deep woods—is vivid.

Experiences like this indwelled me with a deep love of the woods. Every time I enter the forest, my soul slows, my senses quicken, and I feel alive.

But the woods and hunting have never made me feel like a man. Despite doing rugged and "manly" activities in the great outdoors, where real men are supposedly born, it took me learning to be vulnerable to feel like a man.

I've heard men both inside and outside the church say something to the effect of, "Manly men do manly things." Let me put my cards on the table—that's hogwash.

Getting in touch with my inner, wild masculine heart was not a part of my feeling like a man. I've backpacked the Porcupine Mountains of Michigan's Upper Peninsula, the Rocky Mountains of Colorado, near-glaciers in Montana, the end of the Appalachian Trail in Maine, the Grand Canyon of the Tuolumne in California, and along the Bay of Fundy in Nova Scotia. While each was an amazing, adventure-filled experience, and despite all the talk of adventure and wilderness being important for men, they never made me feel like a man.

Truth be told, being in the woods does not make a man a man any more than having sex makes a man a man. What being in the woods will do, like sex, is win admiration from other men. Tell people you went on a weeklong backpacking trip, and watch the reactions. People will be impressed by your feats of survival in the deep wilderness. You may even begin to feel a sense of accomplishment with regard to your masculinity. You've arrived. This has to be the epitome of manliness.

Until you realize women go on solo backpacking trips too.

Two Brothers, Two Men

Early in Genesis, we are introduced to twin brothers, Jacob and Esau. Esau was slightly older than Jacob, but not by much. Jacob came out of their mother's womb right on his heels. Literally. As they grew, the differences between the two brothers grew as well. Esau was a "skillful hunter, a man of the open country, while Jacob was content to stay at home among the tents."[3] Esau was a rugged hunter who liked the wilderness, while Jacob hung out at home with the women and children. On top of that, Jacob was his mother's favorite and was closer to his mother than to his father, who loved Esau more. These two brothers could not be more different.

In our culture, Esau fits the picture of what a man is; Jacob does not. This creates a problem for us as men. Esau is obviously manlier, and yet Jacob is the brother with the greater legacy in the kingdom of God.

If we were to parade Esau and Jacob in front of a group of men and ask who the real man was, how many would choose Jacob? My guess is not many. Christians who argue for a tougher Jesus with biceps and tattoos would love a hairy hunter of a man like Esau and would frown upon a quiet man in the kitchen like Jacob. Jacob's behavior forces us to admit he did not fit modern conceptions of masculinity. Even in the modern church, a man, like Jacob, who stays around women and children and cooks is often rejected for a tougher, calloused, more assertive man.

The story continues, and we are told Esau came in from the open country after a hunt completely famished. Meanwhile, Jacob had been in the kitchen—once again man-failing—cooking some stew.

Starved beyond his senses, Esau demanded that his brother give him some of the stew. Jacob bartered with Esau and traded some stew for his birthright, and because of this, we now refer to the God of Abraham, Isaac, and Jacob—not the God of Abraham, Isaac, and Esau.

But Jacob wrestled with God. That's manly! I think it's fair to say the intent of God's inspired word isn't to make men more manly. But what is the focus? To make men more like Jacob? Quiet men who like to stay near the tents, who don't enjoy the wilderness, and who maybe even like taking responsibility for the cooking chores around camp? Of course not. Creating rigid definitions of masculinity in either direction misses the point. These are the ditches on either side of the road that we must try to avoid.

The book of Romans further complicates the situation by making it clear that God's blessing of Jacob goes beyond Jacob getting the birthright by tricking Esau, or Jacob wrestling with God: "Yet, before the twins were born or had done anything good or bad ... 'Jacob I loved, but Esau I hated.'"[4] God did not choose the manlier man to be the one after whom his chosen people would be named; he chose the quiet one. The one who liked to stay among the tents with women and children. The one who liked to cook. So we have to wonder, *If God would choose Jacob, why frown on this type of man? Why do we continue to look for the Esau archetype?*

More pointedly, was Jacob a failure as a man, or are our stereotypes of men failing us?

No Blank Slates

What gets us into this search for a stereotype? Seeing what we want to see in the biblical text is perhaps the biggest pitfall we face when it comes to reading the Bible. No one is immune to this danger. Seeing what we want to see in the text is what allowed some in previous generations to argue for the legitimacy of slavery. One example of reading into the Bible what we want to see is the prosperity gospel that is prevalent in America. Wanting material wealth, people approach the Scriptures and find a God who will give them their hearts' desire. Seeing only what they want to see, they miss the warnings against being greedy and loving money and claim to have found a God who supports and even encourages their unhealthy desire for material wealth.

Looking at Jacob and Esau and how they fit—or don't fit—our masculine stereotypes, we must ask if we have been defining biblical manhood by what we want to see. When it comes to masculinity, our imaginations have been shaped by Daniel Boone, James Bond, John Wayne, Rocky Balboa, and, in my generation, Jack Bauer. We want our men to be courageous in the face of danger, ruggedly self-sufficient, assertive, and unwilling to back down from a fight. We've grown up with cowboys, astronauts, firemen, and policemen shaping our thoughts on who a man is and what a man does. Hollywood, sports, literature, and even politics shape our fantasies of the quintessential man. This man becomes what sociologists call a "hegemonic masculinity"—a culturally constructed ideal that all men are compared to and encouraged to become. This man shapes our thoughts, ideas, and expectations of what men look like. Because hegemonic ideals are deeply rooted and pervasive in a culture, men and women alike have their imaginations shaped by them.

No one comes to the Bible as a blank slate. Cultural biases, other people's opinions, and even our moods influence how we interpret the Bible. Many Christians believe the Bible is straightforward in what it says and that if you read it, you will be able to clearly determine its meaning. This thinking assumes that an individual's thoughts about politics or gender or sex or money do not affect their interpretation. But these preexisting beliefs are deeply held and are unlikely to be given up quickly.

Modern Christians shake their heads in bewilderment that people could ever use the Bible to justify slavery in America's earliest years. How could people so readily oppress and dehumanize others and rest their consciences on a pillow of Scripture? It is because the cultural argument for slavery had been made, and with those biases, they saw what they wanted to in the Scripture.

Recognizing one's own cultural biases is an important spiritual discipline making it possible for the biblical reader to identify those preexisting beliefs that have been shaped by culture rather than by Scripture. This can be extremely scary. Allowing those beliefs to be challenged by the Word of God can be wildly disorienting as it reorients us around Jesus. This is what Paul meant when he said we must be transformed by the renewing of our minds.[5] We have to be conscious not only of how cultural norms impact our reading of Scripture but also of how our beliefs and worldview impact what we want to see when we read.

For example, if we want to reinforce the macho masculine archetype, it is likely all we will see in the Bible is Samson, King David the warrior, Jesus clearing the temple, and the warrior Jesus of the book of Revelation, and we will miss the quiet, gentle Jacob who hangs around the tents, David the poet and harp player, Gideon scared out of his mind, and the weeping Jesus.

There is tension in our culture with regard to masculinity. Again we take a look at Jacob. Was Jacob not a man when he was around the tents cooking? Did he only become a man after he wrestled with God? Could he have been a man in both instances?

When it comes to understanding what it means to be a man—and a woman, for that matter—we do well to begin with questions. Typically, we are much quicker to give answers than to ask questions. So we are told that men are brash warriors, ready to fight, assertive, and wild. We rarely see the question, *Is that what they should be?*

In Genesis 3, when sin entered the world it fractured everything.

Everything. Our relationship with God, relationship with creation, and our relationship with other humans were all fractured from their once perfect state. Sin affected not only our relationships but every part of our being. Thought patterns, sexuality, desires, and speech all broke upon that initial disobedience. So widespread was the reach of sin that even our natural inclinations were affected. So, yes, men may be brash and wild and ready for a fight from birth, but the question is, *Could that be a result of the fall?* Are all the natural inclinations of men, and again women, good and right? Or like everything else, do they need to be sanctified and redeemed and transformed into a new creation through the Holy Spirit?

Masculinity Affirmed

Every guy needs some experience, some epiphany, or some outside voice to validate his masculinity. There is no formula for this. Some may need to go into the woods to survive for a week by themselves. Some may need to shoot a deer to get in touch with their masculinity. Some may need to build something with their hands. Still others may need to learn how to cry. And that's the point. There is no one way to be a man. Masculinity, like humanness, is wide enough to include many different expressions of manhood. Some men can be the breadwinner, and some men can stay at home with the kids. Some men can fight battles, and some men can write poems. Some men can love the outdoors and tie square knots, and some men can love the indoors and practice feng shui. Being a man is not dependent on what one does; rather, a man is a man because he is made in the image of God. That's it. Focusing masculinity on what a man does makes it something to be proved. Masculinity does not need to be proved; it needs to be affirmed.

My fear is that this effort to challenge men to find the "wild man" has not produced the intended result. Rather than encouraging all men, it encouraged some men while emasculating and alienating others. In order for all men to be encouraged, a broader understanding of masculinity must be embraced—one that is found not in man himself but in the God in whose image he is created. It must not be separate from femininity, nor should it be positioned as superior to femininity. Rather, a true understanding of masculinity will be one that recognizes the complementary nature of the masculine and the feminine as reflections of the God from whom these characteristics derive their expression.

Instead of using superficial standards to define masculinity, we need to understand manhood in more theological terms. We must lose our self-reliance and see ourselves as absolutely dependent on God. United to Christ and confirmed through the Spirit, we are given the new identity of a son of God. This identity shapes our role in the restorative mission of God. Wherever men find themselves—home, work, neighborhood, arts, places of recreation—they become agents of God's kingdom by taking responsibility for the world around them. Abandoning stereotypes of rugged individualism, we are in need of a community of grace and truth. All of this requires men to embrace a posture of humility and vulnerability.

For thirty-one years of my life I worked hard to project an image of being a man. I lifted weights, competitively engaged in sports, hunted, backpacked, downhill skied, and did all the other activities associated with being a man. In social circles, I presented myself as confident, unshakeable, and a leader. Outside of occasionally wearing a pink polo shirt, I presented myself as a man's man. Yet despite all my efforts to embody the cultural definition of a "man," I never felt like I attained the status of "man." It wasn't until I did something that seemed unmanly that I felt like a man.

It was when I had the courage to be vulnerable and let tears wash away the pretense that I began to believe, for the first time in my life, that I was man enough.

CHAPTER 2

MAN MADE

I simply knew, via song, sunlight, redwings, and
cottonwoods, that there was a world I was born
to live in, that the men I was standing beside
lived in another, and that as long as I remembered
this their words would never hurt me again.

David James Duncan

Jake and I never got along. We went to the same church and school, and we even rode the same bus, but despite spending all of this time together, we never came close to being friends. He could be a punk, but I wouldn't categorize him as a bully by any means—in fact, when I look back on it, he was probably bullied and ostracized more than other kids. He was loud and brash, and he could easily be provoked to emotional outbursts, which, as middle school students, we enjoyed watching erupt out of him.

One morning on the way to school, Jake and I got into it on the bus. I'm not sure what started the verbal back-and-forth, but I do remember the outcome. The bus arrived at school, and everyone stood up to get off. Jake was behind me, and there were one or two people standing between us. I turned and said something to provoke him. And Jake did what Jake often did: he got upset.

Then he punched me in the eye.

To understand what happened next, you need to know that in middle school I loved the *Robin Hood* movie starring Kevin Costner. Not because I loved Kevin Costner, but because it was really the first PG-13 movie I was allowed to watch. More importantly, I loved archery, and the movie was full of bows and arrows. I wished I could shoot a bow like Robin Hood.

Early in the movie, just as the conflict between Robin Hood and the sheriff of Nottingham is ramping up, Robin Hood opens a door to find the sheriff and his men waiting to take him prisoner. Not wanting to go down without a fight, Robin Hood grabs his knife and slices the sheriff across the cheek. Fast-forward to the end of the movie. The sheriff and Robin Hood are squaring off for the final sword fight. Robin is not yet ready for the fight, and the sheriff seizes the moment by quickly raising his sword and slicing Robin on the chin. As Robin grabs his chin, the sheriff gestures to his cheek and says, "Now we are even."

After Jake punched me in the eye, I did exactly what the sheriff did: gesturing to my eye, saying, "Now we are even." Don't ask me why I did this. Maybe it was because I was so surprised that I had gotten punched. Maybe I wanted to acknowledge I had provoked him, and I wanted to provoke him a little more but didn't want to get into a full-fledged fight. Maybe because (this is painful to say) I thought it was cool.

Even as I write this, I think the real reason I mimicked that scene is because I didn't want to appear weak. I didn't want to cry. I didn't want to fight. Fighting isn't in my nature. To be completely honest, I've never actually been in a real fight. So I did what came to me: I mimicked an agitator.

But that's not who I am either.

In the moment, it was the best way I knew to act like a man without hitting him back. I knew I didn't want to punch him. That would get me trouble. The gesture was something I could do to show those who were watching that he didn't hurt me. That I could take a punch. Even more, that I was above him because I didn't retaliate. My righteousness would prove my manhood.

I wish the story had ended there, but it didn't. Our bus always got to school early, and before school started, we'd go into the gym and play basketball. By the time I got to the gym, my feelings started getting the best of me, and rather than playing basketball, I sat along the wall and I cried.

I was humiliated. I was hurt—physically and emotionally.

I got punched, and I didn't fight back.

I didn't know the word then, or even the feeling, but I know now. I was emasculated. Technically, "emasculation" refers to complete castration—the removal of the anatomical reason one is a man. But it also refers to a man's loss of virility, power, strength, and spirit.[1] This is what I felt on that day. On the surface, I pretended to be strong and that it didn't bother me that I got punched. But deep down, it hurt. Not just my eye, but my pride. Something told me that my response to Jake was not good enough. Not for others.

So I cried.

Men live in fear of being seen as not-men. It isn't necessarily a fear of being perceived of or thought of as a physical woman. We know there is a biological reality separating us from the opposite gender. No, we do not fear being women; we fear being *likened* to a woman. We fear being effeminate. Limp-wristed. We fear being seen as someone who doesn't respond like a man. We fear being not-men. The only way to prove you are not a not-man is, when the situation requires it, to respond in a way that others will see as manly. No man is exempt from having to prove he is a man. Our culture teaches us that men are not born; men are made. And thus men have to prove they have been made into a man.

Something to Prove

You can be born male in every way: genitals, body structure, strength. However, being born male does not mean you are a man. Not in the eyes of society, and more importantly to men, not in the eyes of other men. The title of "man" must be earned by fulfilling the requirements culture determines necessary to separate boys from men. In some ways, this seems strange and foreign, but inherently all men know they don't just become men; they must be made into a man.

Every society and culture has an approved way for men to be men.[2] In some cultures, you become a man when you pass through some kind of survival initiation. In other cultures, you become a man when you get your own cows or when a boy rejects the care and nurture of his mother by no longer living in her house—finding a wife and proving himself able to care for his family. Here in America, men prove themselves by becoming economically independent, self-made, self-reliant (fix their cars, fix leaky plumbing, kill gophers in the garden), and powerful. Whatever the process, the point is the same: Manhood isn't bestowed on you just because you are genetically male; you must prove yourself worthy of being called a man.

Anthropologist David Gilmore writes, "True manhood is a precious and elusive status beyond mere maleness" and is connected to a deep "inner insecurity that needs dramatic proof." In many cultures, a boy's ability to achieve the status of "man" is "doubtful, resting on rigid codes of decisive action in many spheres of life: a husband, father, lover, provider, warrior. A restricted status, there are always men who fail the test. These are the negative examples, the effete men, the men-who-are-no-men, held up scornfully to inspire conformity to the glorious ideal."[3]

Historically, American men could achieve the status of "man" by passing certain culturally approved tests: success in business or sports, acts of heroism or bravery, exploration, sexual prowess, and displays of political or social power. However, due to changing societal values and the equal rights movement for women, these tests no longer procure masculinity the way they used to—at least not in all sectors of society. America's deep division between Republican and Democrat parallels the deep division in how we think of being male. While somewhat of a caricature, in conservative circles men are still very much thought of as sports-loving, burger-grilling, car-fixing dudes, which is contrasted in liberal circles, where men are seen as educated, interested in the arts, and connoisseurs of fine wine. Anxiety surrounds masculinity, not because it is being lost, but because it is changing, and we aren't sure which definition to use.

New definitions and ideals need to be developed so we as men can express our masculinity in a way that allows us to more authentically be ourselves and live more emotionally rich and meaningful lives. As men, we have for far too long had to prove ourselves as men against aging ideals. And even if we are able to prove ourselves as a man according to the old ideals, to keep the status it must be continually earned.

On the surface, we don't feel or see the anxiety around maintaining our status as a man because it is the water that we swim in. Or to quote an old proverb: "Fish are the last to discover water." Men don't sit around talking about the anxiety they feel to prove themselves. I've never been with a group of guys and had someone say, "You know, I am just exhausted from making sure people see me as a man." This doesn't mean we don't feel the pressure. We do. But we are so accustomed to the pressure that we don't know what it is like to not feel it.

Think about how hard men work to avoid titles like "girly man," "pansy," "sissy," "wimp," "metrosexual," or some other effeminate term. Or conversely, how easily we can be berated into doing ridiculous things by reacting to terms like "chicken" or "scaredy-cat" (I can't help but think of Marty McFly from *Back to the Future* here). The best way for men to challenge their opponent or display their superiority over another is to feminize them in public. One's manhood is constantly under fire and always up for debate.

A good yet stupid example of men proving themselves happened at my bachelor party. Now, I'm not lying when I say I had one of the greatest bachelor parties of all time. Preparation began weeks before the actual party with cryptic notes sent to those attending with instructions to mail "registration fees" to some unknown woman. Phone calls to my fiancée by those planning the party, asking her what parts of me they couldn't hurt during the party. The pregame to the party had every guy invited talking about the party weeks ahead of time. We were all excited. And nervous.

At one point during the party, a couple of guys got into a little one-upmanship. Nothing serious, just a lot of "manly" fun. The end result was that one guy drank what was left of a Costco-sized bottle of salsa, strapped on a life jacket, and swam across the lake and back. Why? Because men don't back down from a challenge. It does not matter how stupid the challenge. It doesn't even matter if everyone knows it is ridiculous. You have to protect your pride—your manhood. Men will cheer when you strap on the life jacket, and they will taunt you until you do. And if you don't chug the salsa, you'll hear about it for the rest of the night. A man's claim to being a man is always under scrutiny.

This is what women often fail to understand. From the outside, it just seems like men are competitive for no reason. What is not understood—often by both women and men—is why men are hard on each other. Our competitiveness is born out of an anxiety we feel about the possibility that others might see us as a not-man. We know that for us to be seen as a man, we have to prove we are one. So even when it seems ridiculous, we strap on the life jacket to prove ourselves to our friends. Earn a certain amount of money. Accomplish that feat. Achieve that title. The need to prove ourselves as a man is a reality, but for those of us in Christ, it is completely unnecessary.

"You Play Ball Like a Girl!"

Proving that you have what it takes to be a man starts early in life. In one of my favorite scenes in the movie *The Sandlot*, we find the sandlot boys on their baseball diamond as a rival group of boys ride up on their bikes. The kids on the bikes are the elite players. The ones who wear uniforms and play organized baseball. They all look the same—clean-cut and athletic. The sandlot boys are misfits. Every boy a different size, mostly unathletic and shaggy.

One of the sandlot boys, Ham Porter, gets into a verbal fight with one of their rivals, Phillips. Back and forth they go with the names. Jerk. Idiot. Moron. Scab eater. Finally, Ham gets pushed too far, and he winds up and delivers a strike: "You play ball like a girl!"

Long before they are adults, the sandlot boys, along with most of us, feel the need to prove their masculinity. Unfortunately, this isn't something we can just do once and then rest in the security of that accomplishment for the rest of our lives. Our masculinity is continually put to the test by measuring ourselves against other men. Relationships with other men are often undergirded by competition and the fear that at any moment we will be found out as weak, timid, or afraid. John Steinbeck captures this reality in his novel *Of Mice and Men* through the voice of Curley's wife.

> "Funny thing," she said. "If I catch any one man, and he's alone, I get along fine with him. But just let two of the guys get together an' you won't talk. Jus' nothin' but mad." She dropped her fingers and put her hands on her hips. "You're all scared of each other, that's what. Ever'one of you's scared the rest is goin' to get something on you."[4]

At first glance, it may seem absurd that men are afraid of each other. But with a little consideration, we can see the truth of Steinbeck's words. Boys will choke back tears so they are not seen as weak. Men will hide being fired from work so as to not be seen as a failure. We work to cover up anything that might be used as evidence to categorize us as one of the men-who-are-no-men. In fact, we go to great lengths to prove ourselves to each other. Visit a locker room and listen to the stories men will weave as evidence of their manliness. As much as we may try to deny it, we long for validation of our masculinity from other men.

A Broader Vision

Every culture has its ideal vision of masculinity. Sociologist Erving Goffman once wrote, "In an important sense there is only one complete unblushing male in America: a young, married, white, urban, northern, heterosexual, Protestant, father, of college education, fully employed, of good complexion, weight, and height, and a recent record in sports ... Any male who fails to qualify in any one of these ways is likely to view himself—during moments at least—as unworthy, incomplete, and inferior."[5]

That was written in 1963, and, by and large, it is still true today. Our definition of what it means to be a man has changed little in the last fifty years. I have had conversations with men who don't feel like men because they are overweight. Once, a young man who started attending our church shared over coffee that he had just graduated from college and now was trying to meet a woman to marry. When I pressed him about this, he told me that getting married was the next step in becoming a man. Another man I know is a stay-at-home dad. After he lost his job, his wife has been the primary financial provider for their family for the last couple of years. While he loves staying home with his kids, he told me the hardest part is when people question him about why he doesn't go get a job. The implication to their question is clear: If you don't provide for your family, you're not man enough.

Cultural ideals of manhood must be challenged because they inherently exclude those who don't—or can't—conform. They rob those men of their manhood. If a man doesn't work to conform to the cultural standards, his manhood is met with a barrage of questions meant to shame him into conformity:

Why are you single?

Why don't you have kids?

Why don't you like sports (or worse, You did theatre?)?

Why are you staying at home while your wife works?

The underlying question is always, *What's wrong with you as a man?*

Our cultural definition of being a man has had a significant impact on our churches' expectations of men. Men are often exhorted from the pulpit to be a leader, be confident, make hard decisions, provide for your family financially, fight battles, be a good father, and love your wife well, because, after all, this is what God says men should do. Many of these are fine things—*if* you have a family. Even in our churches the assumption is that all men get married; all men have kids; and all men are leaders. When you boil it down, there is little difference between Erving Goffman's description of the ideal American man and the American church's ideal man.

The obvious question is, "Who is influencing who?"

One of the great joys of my life is that, on most Sundays during the year, I stand in front of a couple hundred people and proclaim the gospel. I get to look out over the faces of people as they listen to the good news of Jesus. When I look over the congregation I see a myriad of expressions of manhood. I see men who fit the earlier description, and men who don't. Men who are a little heavier, who love ham radio, who are loud, who are quiet, who are leaders, who are not leaders, who are not athletic, who are not married, who are not white, and who are stay-at-home dads.

Are they men? Man enough?

Trying to come up with a single definition of manhood is an exercise in reductionism. It will always fail to include someone or some group, thereby, even if unintentional, pronouncing them not-men. Unfortunately, recent efforts in American Christianity to get men to "act like a man" have been just as alienating for men who already feel inferior against an impossible standard. One man told me about a church men's retreat he attended right out of college. He was young and impressionable, and the man speaking said that men, as good stewards and leaders of their family, don't pay for things they can do for themselves. He went on and on about fixing cars, to the point that the young man left feeling like he would be a lousy husband and father because he couldn't fix a car. To say it more simply, the church, like culture, can measure men against a singular archetype and shame those who fail to conform.

Think back to *The Sandlot*. When the two groups of boys square off, there is a very telling picture. In one group, you have those who are clean-cut, athletic, and elite. They fit the model of being a man. One doesn't have to question their masculinity because you can see it. They are more confident. They walk with their backs straighter. They are more aggressive. Their bodies are better proportioned.

When we look at the sandlot boys, they don't quite fit the picture. Some of them are scrawny. Some of them are overweight. Some wear glasses. Some of them are wearing clothes that don't fit. Many of them aren't even very good at baseball.

While these two groups are just boys at this point, it is easy to see that, as they age, one group will have an easy time proving they are men, and the other group will have a much more difficult time proving they are men, because one group fits the ideal picture of masculinity in our culture. Even American culture, with its proud multicultural mosaic, is not above owning a singular vision of the ideal man—this overarching archetype for all men to strive for—but, like all cultures, demanding that our men conform to our predetermined ideals.

Sons of God

Understanding the gospel news that we are adopted as sons of God who are united to Christ frees us up from the pressure we feel to prove ourselves as men.

Consider some of the men we would hold up as heroes—men whose faith inspires our own. David committed adultery and conspired to have his mistress's husband killed. If there was ever a test to prove one's heart was aligned with the heart of the God who said, "You shall not murder" and "You shall not covet your neighbor's wife,"[6] I'm guessing David would have failed to prove himself worthy. And yet, despite David's unworthiness, God proclaims him worthy of the title "a man after my own heart."[7]

Do you remember when Peter tells Jesus he will go to prison and even die for Jesus? I imagine Jesus smiled kindly at Peter, wrapped his arms around him, and then said, "Peter, I love you. But you are going to disown me three times before the sun rises."[8] And Peter did. He failed to prove himself loyal. Failed to prove he would keep his word. Despite his failure, Jesus reinstates Peter with the responsibility of feeding his sheep.[9]

Paul was the world's greatest missionary. Yet, before his conversion he hunted down Christians and breathed out "murderous threats" against them.[10] In fact, Acts 9 tells us just how far Paul was willing to go to persecute Christians. In verse 1, we're told that Paul went to the high priest and asked for letters to take to the synagogues in Damascus so whenever he found Christians there, he "might take them as prisoners to Jerusalem."[11] While this tidbit seems benign, Paul is actually enacting an old law from a treaty in 142 BC that allowed Israel to extradite refugees from surrounding countries. He is going out of his way to find Christians and bring them to Jerusalem to imprison them. And yet God says, "I deem you worthy to be my apostle to the Gentiles."

God does not require people to prove themselves as worthy before he calls them to himself. Rather, in his calling of people, God deems them as worthy. Do you see how backward that is from what we normally experience? For most of us, experience has taught us that acceptance comes only when we show ourselves worthy of it. I find in my work as a pastor that one of the most common struggles people share with me is wondering how God could ever love them because, in their eyes, they aren't worthy. Aren't good enough. Most feel as if they must do something, prove something, before God could ever love them.

This is the gospel: that we do not need to prove ourselves to God, but rather, by his good, divine choice, God declares us to be his adopted sons and daughters. In his grace and according to his love, God accepts us as sons; he calls us co-heirs with Christ. This unbelievable privilege is made possible through the reconciling death and resurrection of Jesus. Amazing grace it is—that this title, son, is bestowed on us long before we prove ourselves worthy of it. Grace is this—that though we continually relapse into behavior unchar- acteristic of sons of God, we are never declared unworthy of our adoption. Despite having every reason to be, "Jesus is not ashamed to call [us] brothers."[12] It is this good news that allows us to be the men whom God created us to be. Proving oneself to be a man is an anxious endeavor. You never know if you are good enough. Never know if you have done enough. Always left wondering if others are perceiving you to be the man you are working so hard to project.

Always questioning if you are man enough. Our union with Christ unequivocally answers this question in the affirmative.

My father-in-law struggled for years, trying to be the man he thought others wanted him to be. He wasn't an athlete, but he was smart. Wicked smart. He used his intellectual ability to try to prove himself to others. He boasted of his abilities and accomplishments in an attempt to impress those around him. Looking back now, he sees it was a less than effective strategy. Rather than winning the respect and admiration of his peers, he came across as arrogant and almost cavalier. Obviously, this affected nearly all of his relationships in negative ways. And despite his best efforts to fix the damage he was doing, nothing worked.

A few years after he came to faith in Christ, he began to question his salvation and wrestle through a dark night of the soul. God felt distant. My father-in-law felt alone. In his own words, he said, "I lost my confidence." When I asked him about this, he said he would go to work, and where he once acted confidently and played the role of a man who had it all together, he no longer could do that. He would watch his coworkers and wonder how they kept the pretense going, because now, suddenly, he no longer could.

Through a series of events, God brought my father-in-law to a place where he cried out to him. He gave up his best efforts to control things and simply asked that God would move. That request proved to be life-changing. God revealed grace. Love. And my father-in-law was never the same.

Within a year, my father-in-law stepped down from his position as chairman of the council of ministries—a role that had been a source of pride and one where he thought that people saw him as the man he wanted to be—and found himself serving in the children's ministry at church. For thirty-one years, he and my mother-in-law led children's ministries at the churches they belonged to. Though he served in a ministry men didn't typically become involved in, he felt no shame, no uneasiness, about serving in this way. In fact, he tells a story of a time when he was being exceptionally goofy with the children when a deacon came in to check on how things were going. While the deacon watched, the thought flashed through my father-in-law's mind of how ridiculous he must look—a grown man letting go of all self-consciousness and decorum to connect with three- and four-year-olds. But he realized he didn't care. This was what he was called to do.

This is the power of the gospel. You are a son of God. A brother of Jesus. You have been called according to the good purpose of God. While this may not shore up your masculinity in the eyes of other men, it should give you the confidence to be who you are. Not who culture wants you to be. Not who others goad you into being. Freed by this gospel, you don't have to force yourself into some pretense so you measure up. Be who you are. That's who God created. You are "God's handiwork, created in Christ Jesus to do good works, which God prepared in advance" for you to do.[13]

Make Every Effort

Certain passages in the Bible at first glance seem to suggest we *do* need to prove ourselves. However, upon further examination, we find they are lined thick with grace. In Luke 13, Jesus is asked if only a few people are going to be saved. He responds by saying, "Make every effort to enter through the narrow door, because many, I tell you, will try to enter and will not be able to. Once the owner of the house gets up and closes the door, you will stand outside knocking and pleading, 'Sir, open the door for us.'"[14] On the surface, this verse seems to imply we must prove ourselves to Jesus by our effort to enter the narrow door.

I have long wrestled with what Jesus meant when he said, "Make every effort." How do you know when you have made enough effort to get in? Getting into heaven or the kingdom of God is often presented as an easy thing that requires almost no effort. Raise your hand, sign a card, come down to the altar, get in the water—that's all you have to do. But it seems like Jesus is saying the exact opposite. That getting in, or being accepted by God, requires effort. How does this square with the gospel discussed earlier, where God accepts us and deems us worthy before we give him our best efforts?

A while back, my community group at church wrestled with this very text from Luke. For quite some time, we talked about the possibilities of what Jesus meant, and as the conversation went around and around, I noticed a trend in the responses. It wasn't always explicit, but lying just beneath what almost everyone said was feelings of guilt or of not doing enough to "enter through the narrow door." And then it struck me.

What if "making every effort" is doing the hard work of believing we are accepted and loved by God as a son or daughter right now? What if "making every effort" is the effort it takes to drown out culture's voice, which says we need to prove ourselves? What if "making every effort" is the difficult task of holding on to the "grace upon grace" that calls us beloved?[15]

This isn't an effort to soften the words of Jesus. Quite the contrary. Learning to accept grace is one of the hardest things a person can do. For most people, it is easier to believe the negative about ourselves than it is to believe the positive. When we are constantly told we are not good enough, resting in being loved as we are becomes a nearly impossible task. It truly does take "every effort" to stop thinking there must be something else required of us, something else we have to do to prove ourselves. It takes every effort to stop, and just accept grace.

Some of us are caught in the fruitless pursuit of making every effort to prove our manliness. We exude a macho persona, not because that's who we are or who we want to be, but because it is what we think is necessary to be seen as a man.

Even in the eyes of God.

Some of us exhaust ourselves to provide for our families, even if it means ignoring our kids, so we can "be the man" we think we are supposed to be. Others of us are emotionally aloof, adopting a steely resolve because "that's what a man does." We tell our boys to "man up" in the face of difficult situations, even if it implicitly teaches them that if a situation gets the best of them, if they get scared, or if they get hurt, they fail at being men. We do this because this is all we know about being a man. Prove yourself. Measure up. Man up. But in all these ways, we are communicating to our boys and men that they must break their necks trying to be seen as a man. And in our demands, we are contradicting the good news that God has freed them from the oppressive prison of an unattainable, unnatural standard.

Rather than trying to prove our masculinity, we need to accept who we are in the spirit of the gospel. Instead of trying to live up to some cultural standard of manhood, we need to accept God's grace, which says, "I accept you just as you are." It is culture, not God, that alienates those who do not live up to the existing, narrow definition of manhood.

Before we men can ever rest in our masculinity, we must first rest in the grace of God. Whether or not we've proved ourselves worthy of the title, God adopts us as sons. Like the prodigal son who has returned home, the heavenly Father places his signet ring on our finger to communicate our status in his household. We belong. Once this son understands that God does not require proof to gain acceptance but simply loves him for who he is, then the son can begin to rest in his masculinity. We men can begin to live out of our true selves. No longer is there any need to prove it, because we are already accepted. As one reborn in Christ, a man is made new and already deemed worthy.

Or to say it another way, you are already man enough.

CHAPTER 3

SHIFTING SANDS

The problem with most self-made men is
that they often worship their creator.

Unknown

When my wife was pregnant with our first child, we decided we didn't want to know the sex of the baby. We were going to do childbirth old school and find out when the doctor held up the gooey, little bundle of joy. While we were excited about our decision to not utilize all of the technology of modern medicine, the decision to not know the sex made nesting and baby showers a royal pain. These days, everything baby is coded in gender-specific colors and pictures. Blue clothing with trains and animals on it, bedding with flowers and pink ribbons, and mobiles with footballs or princesses—everything is connected to gender. I dare you to try to find gender-neutral clothing at Babies "R" Us.

It wasn't always this way. Prior to the 1880s, all babies were dressed in gender-neutral clothes until early childhood. At the turn of the century, this began to change. People sought to dress their infants and toddlers in gender-appropriate clothing, sparking a debate that raged across the country: Pink or blue? Which color goes with which sex?

A 1918 editorial in the magazine *Infants' Department* sought to settle the debate once and for all: "There has been a great diversity of opinion on the subject, but the generally accepted rule is pink for the boy and blue for the girl. The reason is that pink being a more decided and stronger color is more suitable for the boy, while blue, which is more delicate and dainty, is prettier for the girl."[1]

Well, that settles it.

This clearly shows what we have been saying up to this point: What is normative for a person's gender is largely determined by culture, and these norms change as the culture changes.

Defining what it means to be a man is tricky because, in reality, there is not one definition of masculinity; there are many definitions of masculinity. Many would have us believe there is a universal ideal of masculinity, that there is one way to be a man in the world. These same people are the ones who would have us believe that masculinity is under attack in America. They feel as though men can no longer be men but are being feminized by the world around them. Anyone who is deemed too feminine — liberals, women, homosexuals, educated, Europeans, stay-at-home dads — are pegged as the enemy working for the destruction of not only the American male but American society as a whole. Listen to them long enough, and you might be tempted to place manliness on an endangered species list because of the threat it faces.

Masculinity is not under crisis because of feminizing, but it is in trouble because it is, more often than not, defined by what it is not rather than by what it is. Real men don't cry. Real men don't back down from a fight. Real men don't cheat on their wives. Defining itself by what it is not results in an insecure machoism that attacks anything it deems to be a threat to its own masculinity.

The definition of manhood shifts like the sand on a beach. Its contours, edges, and form bend, soften, harden, and grow according to the changing needs and demands of society. For example, during wartime, the ideal man is a soldier, rifle in hand, cigarette hanging from his lips — all strength and swagger. After the war, it's the guy carrying a lunch box and wielding a wrench or a welding torch in a factory. He makes things with his hands. Unless you live in Texas. Then the ideal man still has a rifle in his hand. In the city, it is Don Draper with his tailored suits, corner office, and business acumen. In high school, the manly guy plays football. In college, he belongs to the right fraternity. In the neighborhood, he drives the best car. As the criteria for manhood shifts, we are pressured to shift with it.

Applying a universal ideal of masculinity ignores the multiple masculinities always present in society. Despite our awareness of the different types of men out there, many of us anxiously wonder if we are doing enough to be a man. If the dominant ideal is a Don Draper, a mechanic may not feel like he is enough. Compared to a cowboy in Texas, an accountant may feel like less of a man. To alleviate this anxiety, we must broaden our understanding of what it means to be a man.

Called to One Image

As Christians, we rightly turn to the Bible for guidance, usually landing at 1 Timothy 3 and Titus 1, where the qualifications of an elder are laid out by Paul. Elders, being men worth imitating, are often seen as the benchmark for a real Christian man:

- above reproach
- faithful to his wife
- temperate
- self-controlled
- respectable
- hospitable
- gentle
- good managers of the family
- lovers of good
- upright
- holy
- disciplined
- holding firmly to the truth of the faith

This is a great list of characteristics for men to embody. All of these are Christ exalting and Christ glorifying. But outside of "faithful to his wife" and, for some, "good managers of the family," this is a list of characteristics women should seek to embody as well ("good managers of the family" may be taken off the list if your theology of gender roles is more egalitarian). Don't we believe that Christian women should be above reproach? Self-controlled? Lovers of good? The inherent danger of equating some Christlike characteristics with masculinity but not with femininity is that we fail to engage women in discipleship that calls them and sanctifies them into the image of Christ. Discipleship and imitating Christ are not just male endeavors but are the work of all followers of Jesus—male and female.

I don't say all of this to call into question what the biblical ideal of a man is, nor is it my intent to offer up some genderless Christianity. Rather, my hope is that men and women are encouraged to grow into these good and right biblical characteristics apart from a culturally constructed gender ideal. For example, is there room in the church for a man to be gentle in a way that is true to his personality without being seen as an effeminate version of a man? Can a man hate violence and be a pacifist and still be considered a man in the church? Can a man not fight back without having to prove in other ways that he is a man? Can a man enjoy the arts, be moved to tears by music, be present to his emotions, and soft with his words and still be thought of as a man?

The fact that we have to ask these questions shows that even in the church, there are strict expectations placed on men regarding how they talk, think, and feel.

As I wrote earlier, all of us see through a particular lens when we come to the Bible. We come with a worldview, some of which has been shaped by the culture around us, and we interpret the text through those lenses. So just how have the historical shifts in American masculinity shaped our understanding of what the Bible says about men?

Rise of the Breadwinner

American sociologist Michael Kimmel's academic career has focused on gender, and his extensive overview, *Manhood in America*, helped me understand these major shifts in American masculinity.

Prior to the American Revolution, manhood in America looked very European. Being a man meant owning land, being a strong moral authority at home, having a high level of civic involvement, and holding to Christian morals (even if not necessarily being a professing Christian). The majority of America's founding fathers — George Washington, Thomas Jefferson, John Adams, for example — fit this description.

But the American Revolution birthed not only a new America but a new man.[2] During the American Revolution, the definition of manhood shifted and mirrored the separation and independence of America from Britain. Rather than being defined by owning land and embodying certain values, a man began to be seen as someone who was independent, useful, heroic, and industrious. It was during this time — between 1810 and 1820 — that *breadwinner* originated as a term to define the role of men in society and the family.

The idea of a breadwinner has remained central to what it means to be a man. If one can provide for his family, then he is a man. If he cannot — if he fails, is unemployable, or shirks his responsibility — then he is looked on by society and the church as less of a man.

This is incredibly shame producing for those men who cannot or do not provide for their families. I have heard many stories from stay-at-home dads who have had 1 Timothy 5:8 — "Anyone who does not provide for their relatives, and especially for their own household, has denied the faith and is worse than an unbeliever" — thrown in their face because their wives are out working. To say that any Christian is worse than an unbeliever is not something we should take lightly. Should it really be applied to stay-at-home dads? Before we go out and make such damning accusations, we must look at the context of this verse to make sure we are using it appropriately.

Starting at verse 3:

> Give proper recognition to those widows who are really in need. But if a widow has children or grandchildren, these should learn first of all to put their religion into practice by caring for their own family and so repaying their parents and grandparents, for this is pleasing to God. The widow who is really in need and left all alone puts her hope in God and continues night and day to pray and to ask God for help. But the widow who lives for pleasure is dead even while she lives. Give the people these instructions, so that no one may be open to blame. Anyone who does not provide for their relatives, and especially for their own household, has denied the faith and is worse than an unbeliever.[3]

Even a quick reading of the surrounding verses causes one to realize that Paul is not talking about gender roles at all. Paul's intent is not to make sure all Christian husbands for all generations take on the primary role of breadwinning. To read this into the passage is to miss the point. Paul's intent is to see that families take primary responsibility for caring for their widowed relatives. He is exhorting the immediate family of a widow to rise to the occasion and take care of their own family so as to not place undue burden on the church. To imply that Paul is making the case for men being the primary breadwinners is to change the most apparent meaning of the text.

Second, verse 8 is addressed to "anyone," not just men. In the Greek, the pronouns throughout the verse take their lead from the first pronoun, which is not gender specific. Many English translations use the "he" and "his" pronouns, but it is more accurate to read them as "they" and "their." This is not about the men's role but about the role of the family.

I'm not trying to come up with some new reading of the text to support my thesis. I'm trying to recover a very old and primary reading of the text. In fact, in his commentary on 1 Timothy (specifically on 1 Timothy 5:8), John Calvin noted that Erasmus, a contemporary of Martin Luther, translated the verse to apply only to women: "If any woman do not provide for her own." Calvin could not embrace a translation where only women were exhorted to care for family because he believed this teaching carried greater weight "if it apply both to men and to women."[4]

This should give us pause and make us wonder if the use of this verse to support male breadwinning is more about a cultural ideal being read into the passage than it is about a biblical mandate.

The problem with making this verse about men being the primary financial earners for their families is that even Jesus would not live up to this ideal. Jesus was not the primary breadwinner for his family. With Joseph no longer in the family picture, the responsibility of caring for the family, and especially for Mary, would have fallen on Jesus as the oldest son. But Jesus wasn't earning a living. He himself noted that "the Son of man has no place to lay his head."[5] Luke's gospel goes so far as to note that it was women who financially supported Jesus and the disciples.[6]

While Jesus did not provide for his family financially, he did provide. Hanging on the cross, Jesus lovingly looked at his mother and said, "Woman, here is your son," and then he looked at his disciple John and said, "Here is your mother."[7] Jesus is looking after his mother's well-being at the time of his death, ensuring that her needs will be provided for.

Looking at Jesus' example, it becomes clear that men can support their families in a number of ways beyond just providing for them financially. A father who stays at home with his children while his wife goes to work is providing care, protection, and presence for them. He is providing, by empowering his wife to work outside the home, for the financial well-being of his family. He is providing opportunity for his wife to fulfill her vocation and use the gifts given to her by God. Is he directly responsible for the financial provision of his family? No. But anyone who says he is not providing for his family has a severely limited understanding of not only what a man can provide but also what a family needs from a man.

Shifting Expectations

The American separation from Europe shifted the defining lines in the sand of masculinity. In Europe, a man's place in society was often determined by his family. There was a social hierarchy, and everyone knew where they stood in society because of their family's position. But in America, there was no heritage to determine a man's place. Social order was no longer something passed down from generation to generation, but one could assume whatever social standing he wanted. Everyone had equal opportunity to achieve a new social standing. In the presence of equals, a man could separate himself through diligence, competitiveness, and hard work. Being able to climb the social ladder and reinvent oneself is the alluring dream of America.

But the ability to redefine one's social standing created a crisis for the identity of men. As historian Charles Sellers wrote, "Sons had to compete for elusive manhood in the market rather than grow into secure manhood by replicating their fathers."[8] Family social standing no longer meant anything. It was not a securing presence in the life of men; rather, it was an obstacle to be overcome. If one worked hard enough, was man enough, he could utilize the market to better his social standing. The market, with its competition and payoffs, became the new proving ground for men.

However, putting the identity of men into the hands of the volatile and insecure marketplace resulted in a masculinity that was restless, insecure, striving, and competitive.[9] The demands of proving one's manhood in the market were so great that Henry David Thoreau referred to it as the "site of humiliation."[10]

A volatile market that could not be controlled became the place where men had to prove themselves. If the wilderness was cruel, the market was crueler. Men were pitted against other men, and rather than experiencing intimacy and camaraderie with other men, they found themselves in constant competition with men. Rather than working together to make the kill, men began killing each other. The drive for economic success was so high that, for most men, the fear of failure nearly drove them mad.

The result of the competition and anxiety is that men became focused on self-control and escape. If they couldn't control the very thing holding their identity as men, then they would either control everything around them or would run from them. As Michael Kimmel notes, "American men chose both."[11]

Drinking became an easy way for men to escape their plight in the marketplace. Because of economic uncertainty, market volatility, and the fortunes being won and lost, between 1790 and 1830, Americans drank more than at any other time in history,[12] and they did it "out of the anxieties of their condition."[13]

Another way men escaped the humiliation of the marketplace was to flee civilization and go west to the untamed wilderness. Daniel Boone, Davy Crockett, and Kit Carson became mythical heroes of the American man. They represented real men who separated themselves from the emasculation of civilization and conquered the natural world through their masculine instincts. Hordes of men followed suit, and for those who couldn't, the myth of the natural man grew.

Escaping the demands of masculinity is still prevalent in men today. But rather than escaping west, men now escape to golf courses, football games, man caves, and gyms—whatever will provide a place where a man can feel like a man.

Not only did men want to escape the marketplace, but they began to escape the home as well. Nearly every society and culture in history has had a division of labor between men and women, regardless of whether the society is a hunter/gatherer or an agricultural society. But no society had a divide as prominent as America's. Alexis de Tocqueville was one of the first people to come to America and extensively study American culture. He noted, "In America, more than anywhere else in the world, care has been taken to constantly trace clearly the distinct spheres of action of the two sexes, and both are required to keep in step, but along paths that are never the same."[14] As men felt less like men at work, at least they could feel like a man in their home.

The lines grew starker at the turn of the century as the tasks men performed around the house—gathering fuel, processing grain, working with leather—no longer needed to be done. Economic success allowed someone else to be paid to do these things, or technological advances eliminated them all together. The result was that the home became entirely the domain of wives. While the wives' chores still needed to be done, husbands found freedom to be less involved in the affairs of the home than ever before.

During this time, scientific, medical, and theological evidence surfaced that "proved" women were biologically inferior than men and theologically exempted from the public sphere. These doctrines were so deeply ingrained in the mind of the culture that de Tocqueville noted that "the independence of woman is irrecoverably lost in the bonds of matrimony: if an unmarried woman is less constrained [in America] than elsewhere, a wife is subjected to stricter obligations."[15] In other words, marriage confined women to the home so men could go out and be men.

In the modern era, gender roles are again a subject of intense conversation. But rather than being a conversation in society, the role of women is a conversation in the church. American culture has moved, and is moving, to embrace women's rights in politics, work, and even sports. But in the church, this separation of spheres—men have their role and women have their role, and they are separate—is, in some churches, still in place. One has to wonder how the strict separation of roles created by an anxious masculinity has impacted our theological ideas about the role of men and women.

For example, those who argue for the separate roles of men and women often point to Genesis 3 to confirm their beliefs. After Adam and Eve sinned, God pronounced judgments that would affect the rest of their lives. Adam has his work, and the ground he works is cursed. Eve's judgment affects her childbearing, so it is made painful. Some view these as separate judgments over the separate spheres of life for which the two genders are primarily responsible.

There are a number of problems with this interpretation, but we will look at two. First, nowhere does the Bible say that women are to be the primary caregivers of children. Not in Genesis 3; not in the rest of the Bible. In fact, when Paul writes in his letter to the Ephesians, "Fathers, do not exasperate your children; instead, bring them up in the training and instruction of the Lord,"[16] he is encouraging men to play a prominent role in the raising of their children. This is especially important since the push to create separate spheres for men and women resulted in fathers who were increasingly absent from the house as they worked to prove their manhood through tireless striving to earn a bigger paycheck. Absent from the home, fathers left the raising of children to mothers, and sons were abandoned by fathers who worked to conquer the market.

This is confusing, because this is what men are constantly told to do. "Go, be the breadwinner! Provide enough for your family so your wife can stay at home and raise the kids. This is biblical," we tell our men. And then we turn around and bemoan the state of masculinity. "Men are absent from their homes. Boys don't have good role models because their fathers have abandoned them." "Fathers need to step up and not shirk their responsibility around the home," is the cry of many American pastors on Father's Day. Is it any wonder so many men are angry in our society? They can't win.

My friend Ben is a self-employed Realtor who lives in this tension. A father of young children, he longs to be home with them more, but because he works on commission, at times has to put in long hours. He wants to volunteer in his kids' school, take his son fishing during the day, and have tea parties with his daughter. Over drinks one night, he lamented, like we all do, that his kids are growing up so fast. "I want to be with them more," he said, "but work won't allow it. I have to work to provide for them, but I just feel so guilty that I'm gone so often." Many of us are caught in this catch-22. We are either failing to provide enough for our family and need to work longer and harder, or we aren't being with our family enough.

Stark separation between the roles of men and women contributes to the environment where men perpetually fail. Providing clearer delineations between the roles of men and women, as many are trying to do, isn't going to help. We need to see what is written in Scripture very clearly. Simply put, it is not good for a man to be alone and to try to do it all by himself; nor is it good for a woman to be alone and to try to do it all by herself. This is why God made the woman as a helper. A helper is not a secondary position; rather, it is an acknowledgment that we cannot do life alone.

Both Genesis 1 and 2 provide accounts of creation. Genesis 1 creates a rhythmic cadence of God creating and calling it good. Light, and it was good. Plants, and it was good. Creatures, and it was good. And then the rhythm breaks. God creates man and woman and it is very good. Creation is complete. And it is good.

Genesis 2 does not give us this rhythm. God creates all there is, and in a distinctively different manner, he creates man first. There is no woman — just a solitary man in a garden filled with animals. After the man names all the animals, God sees it is not good for Adam to be alone, and thus he creates Eve.

My question is, When in the Genesis 2 account was creation deemed good by God? Before or after the creation of woman?

It seems we have to say it was after the creation of woman, because God deemed something in creation to be not good, namely, man being alone.

We are not meant to be alone. It is not good for us. We need each other, and we need the help of others. The stewardship of creation requires that we do the work together. Men and women helping each other, because it is not good for us to be alone. So together we care for the house. Together we parent our kids. Together we watch over the spiritual condition of our homes. Together we provide and steward, because it is not good for us to be alone.

A second point from the creation narrative: While God declares judgment on Adam and pronounces a curse on the ground, he is not implying that only men are to work the fields. Within God's pronouncement of the curse on the ground, we find this oft quoted verse:

> "By the sweat of your brow
> you will eat your food
> until you return to the ground,
> since from it you were taken;
> for dust you are
> and to dust you will return."
>
> Genesis 3:19

Aren't both men and women to return to dust? Death is the fate of all, regardless of gender.

On top of that, the Bible shows many women who are working in the fields. When Jacob arrives in Paddan Aram, he discovers that Rachel, his future wife, is a shepherd.[17] She isn't spending her time at home, but she is out in the fields tending the sheep. Ruth goes out into the fields and harvests food for herself and Naomi.[18] The woman of Proverbs 31 "considers a field and buys it" and "out of her earnings ... plants a vineyard." She "sees that her trading is profitable," "makes linen garments and sells them," and "supplies the merchants with sashes."[19]

Maybe the separation of spheres between men and women and their role in home and society are marked more by cultural ideals than biblical commands.

A Different Kind of Man

The constant morphing of masculinity is troublesome for those who believe there is one definition of masculinity. Shifts like these have occurred in nearly every generation of American men, with the result that fathers look at their sons and their sons' friends and say, "Kids these days." Fathers sense that their sons are failing to live into what it means to be a man. And that may be entirely the case! It may be that sons are not living into the idea of masculinity that their fathers had to embody, but it isn't because they are less masculine; it's because the standards are changing.

Already in the 1940s, anthropologist Margaret Mead could sense the pressure to measure up to outdated models of masculinity placed on young men:

> Has the American scene shifted so that we still demand of every child a measure of success which is actually less and less possible for him to attain? . . . Have we made it a condition of success that a man should reach a position higher than his father's when such an achievement (for the many) is dependent upon the existence of a frontier and an expanding economy?[20]

I remember the first time I consciously thought about how much money I would earn in my life compared to my dad. Right out of college, I became a youth pastor and made a whopping $25,000 a year. Not bad in youth pastor terms, and considering that I wasn't married and didn't have any kids, it was all I needed. It covered my rent, paid for my sporty Pontiac Grand Prix (it had leather seats!), and allowed me independence. What more could I need?

And then I got engaged.

I started thinking about all the expenses coming up—a house, kids, insurance—and then I looked at my salary and realized it wasn't going to cut it. So I enrolled in seminary. I know, not the most spiritual reason to enroll in seminary, but it is the honest reason. God worked his plan for me to be in seminary and ultimately to become a pastor by appealing to my material desire for stuff. Seminary was a step to economic stability with absolutely zero aspirations of ever being a pastor of adults (let alone a lead pastor). I knew if I got my master of divinity degree, I would be able to earn enough money to support my family. And while the degree would make it easier, I realized I would never be able to provide for my children what my father provided for his.

My mom didn't have to work when we were growing up. We went on extended, two-week vacations traveling the American West. Almost every spring break, we took a weeklong family trip to Colorado to go skiing. We had a boat on Lake Michigan and a family cabin in northern Michigan. You get the idea. My dad earned enough money for us to enjoy a very comfortable middle-class life.

I've often had to confront my frustration that I won't be able to provide my family with those same things. Don't get me wrong: I know I'm called to ministry. I know it is exactly what I'm supposed to do, and that I would be unhappy doing anything else. My gifts, attitudes, and aptitudes, along with affirmation from the church, confirm my call and vocation. And I know ministry is not a place to get rich. But I still wrestle with not being able to provide for my family like my father provided for his, because I have, right or wrong, associated masculinity with an ability to provide.

The truth is, pastor or not, I am a part of the first generation of children in American history who will likely not earn more than their parents. For so long, earning power was a test of masculinity in America. The more you earn, the manlier you are. But that likely will not be true for our children, which compels us to help our sons find new ways to be men. We have to help them see that there are, in fact, many ways to be men. We have to expand the definition of manhood beyond roles and earning power to something much more Christ-centered.

It is time to stop defining masculinity by what men do and start defining it by who men are. It is time to stop pushing men to fulfill a role and start focusing on helping men become human. Rather than focusing on making men breadwinners, warriors, or even better husbands, it is time to focus on encouraging men to be fully human and fully alive. If men can learn to be courageous—and not a "run into a burning house" courageous but a "be authentic about who you are" courageous—then men will be better husbands, better fathers, better coworkers, better neighbors, better friends. Better humans. Embodying characteristics such as vulnerability, integrity, gentleness, and courage will serve men far better in a changing world than forcing them to accept some predetermined role.

Perhaps if we embrace the idea that there are many ways to be a man, men might be free.

CHAPTER 4

MUSCULAR CHRISTIANITY

Jesus was no dough-faced, lick-spittle proposition.
Jesus was the greatest scrapper that ever lived.

Billy Sunday

In 1832, Francis Trollope wrote that he'd never seen a country "where religion had so strong a hold upon women or a slighter hold upon the men" than the United States.[1] Since that time, people have been trying to figure out why so many men avoid church. According to the Pew Forum on Religion and Public Life, every major Christian tradition in the United States has more female members than male; this is mirrored in worship attendance.[2] One study found that in every age bracket, there are more women (61 percent) than men (39 percent) in worship (it's worth noting that some have speculated that the early church also attracted more women than men).[3] Theories on reasons have ranged from effeminate music to the décor of bathrooms to the lack of full beards.

I can't help but wonder if men aren't crossing the threshold of the church because the message of the gospel conflicts with the cultural message guys hear every day. According to cultural definitions of maleness, men must be independent, self-reliant, able to provide, and strong. The gospel tells us we must be dependent on Christ and on other believers, that God is the true provider, and that when we are weak, then we are strong. Maybe men aren't coming to church because it's exhausting to process two contradictory messages. Maybe men aren't coming because if they accept the gospel, then culture won't see them as a man, but if they prove their masculinity in the culture, then they will be racked with guilt at church.

Either way, men can't win.

About the time Francis Trollope wrote that religion in America had a looser grip on men than women, another theory arose to explain why men were avoiding the church. Jesus wasn't manly enough. No, it wasn't that Jesus himself wasn't manly enough; it was the way that Jesus was portrayed. Paintings of Jesus often depicted a doe-eyed, soft-featured, effete-looking man—not someone men could relate to, let alone follow. It was, in all honesty, a horrible mischaracterization of the God man.

Enter muscular Christianity. Billy Sunday was perhaps the most famous of the American preachers who promoted a robust, masculine Jesus. Sunday was a former baseball player who used uncompromising language in his efforts to transform the feminized Christian religion. He preached fiery sermons that reinforced strength and resolve. Christians, according to Sunday, cannot be a sort of "dishrag proposition, a wishy-washy, sissified sort of galoot that lets everybody make a doormat out of him." Sunday viewed church scholars as "anemic rank skeptics" and intellectuals were "fudge-eating mollycoddles." Protestant pastors, in his mind, had become "pretentious, pliable mental perverts," and so Sunday prayed, "Lord, save us from off-handed, flabby-cheeked, brittle-boned, weak-kneed, thin-skinned, pliable, plastic, spineless, effeminate, ossified, three-karat Christianity."[4]

The origins of muscular Christianity can be traced to Victorian England. Two authors, Charles Kingsley and Thomas Hughes, each wrote novels promoting a hearty manliness infused with Christian ideals. In Hughes's novel, *Tom Brown at Oxford*, the narrator summarizes the thought of muscular Christianity:

> [It is] a good thing to have strong and well-exercised bodies ... The least of the muscular Christians has hold of the old chivalrous and Christian belief, that a man's body is given him to be trained and brought into subjection, and then used for the protection of the weak, the advancement of all righteous causes, and the subduing of the earth which God has given to the children of men.[5]

The goal of the movement was to re-masculinize Jesus and the church. The vision put forth in *Tom Brown at Oxford* is a good vision of masculinity. Our bodies *should* be under the submission of Christ.

We *should* work for the advancement of righteous causes, using whatever resources we have to bring about the realization of those causes. We *should* protect the weak. These endeavors are good and right. But the language, and the overemphasis on manliness, made the ideas of the movement ripe for abuse.

According to the muscular Christianity movement, if Christianity were going to survive, Jesus would have to be recast as a man who men not only would relate to but would willingly follow as well. The problem with militant portrayals of Jesus is that they can quickly and easily be co-opted to endorse the subjugation of those deemed less than masculine—whether that is expressed through racism, sexism, or homophobia. For example, the Ku Klux Klan co-opted themes from the muscular Christianity movement for their own sinister purposes, emphasizing Christ as "a robust, toil-marked young man" who "purged the temple with a whip" to further their hateful agenda.[6]

In the bigger picture, the voice of Billy Sunday and the muscular Christianity movement lives on today, almost one hundred years later, reincarnated in popular preachers as they bemoan how the church has transformed Jesus into a "Richard Simmons, hippie, queer Christ," and a "neutered and limp-wristed popular Sky Fairy of pop culture that ... would never talk about sin or send anyone to hell."[7]

While Jesus was not afraid of confrontation and did not mind offending people, muscular Christianity and its proponents offer a depiction of Jesus that is no more accurate than the Swedish, doe-eyed Jesus staring dreamily into the heavens. Representing Jesus as a bravado-filled, muscle-bound male stereotype forces him into a caricature that looks more like a moral version of the typical U.S. male than it does the Jesus of Nazareth who told Peter to put away his sword.

If men have been worrying about an overly effeminate Jesus for more than two hundred years, we have to wonder, *Are we feminizing Jesus, or are we uncomfortable with a Jesus who challenges our cultural definition of what it means to be a man?*

Jesus Laughing

I have a picture of Jesus hanging on the wall in my office. It is a simple picture with very few colors in it. Black, brown, grey, and a little bit of green and blue scattered here and there make up the color spectrum of this simple sketch. Jesus is pictured from the shoulders up, and what attracts me to this picture is the image of Jesus' head thrown back, with his eyes closed and his mouth open in unrestrained laughter.

Jesus laughing. I love it.

I typically disdain pictures of Jesus. I find them hokey. Too often they portray Jesus as expressionless, staring off strangely into some distant horizon, probably heaven, looking apathetic about being on earth as he stands rigidly among a crowd of people. There is a backlit glow that seems to follow him everywhere and causes his hair to shine and his Swedish features to look just a little feminine or androgynous.

But this picture is different. This picture is human.

Sometimes I look at the picture and imagine what would have made Jesus throw his head back and laugh so hard. Maybe it was the children who ran to him, jumping and wrapping their arms around him, nearly knocking him over. Maybe Jesus and the disciples were walking along the road, and one of them said, "Remember that time James and John wanted to rain down fire from heaven? That was silly!" Maybe it was simply sitting with his friends around a table, and the conversation went as conversations go, and everyone was laughing. Maybe a sinner made an inappropriate joke. Maybe Jesus was laughing at his disciples' faces when he walked through the wall and then later ate some fish with them.

This picture is striking to me because, contrary to all of the cultural norms I've been taught about manhood, Jesus' face is full of emotion. He isn't stoic; his face is filled with a joy that cannot be contained. The closed eyes and wide smile suggest a comfort and freedom with expressing his emotions. Everything this picture stirs up in me is extremely human. In every one of the possible reasons for the laughter, I can relate — and this blows my mind — to God through the very human Jesus. This is the beauty and the profundity of the incarnation. It is not only that God can relate to us, but that we can relate to God. His experiences are our experiences, and our experiences are his experiences. The holy otherness of the ineffable God became tangible and describable in the humanity of Jesus.

And yet, because Jesus is so fully human, because he embraced all there is about being human and lived perfectly, he is off-putting. You see, I don't know what to do with a man who can so easily and quickly dine with drunks and prostitutes and teach in synagogues. I've spent so much of my life making sure I hang out with the right people so I can be seen by others as the man I'm supposed to be. For far too long, my concern for who I'm spending my time with has had little to do with loving others but everything to do with protecting my image. Imagine if, in this day and age, a well-known Christian pastor was regularly having dinner with prostitutes and IRS agents. How quick before the news media and Twitter tweeters tromp on the inappropriate behavior of this Bible teacher? I wonder if I, as a pastor of a church, would still have a job if a prostitute were to wash my feet with her hair? Would I be given any benefit of the doubt? Or would I immediately be disgraced as a sexual deviant?

I love my church, but I am confident that if this were to happen, I'd be sitting at a table with my elders answering some questions.

Jesus was so willing to invite scandalous people into his life that people were offended by his associations. So, on the one hand, we have this amazingly gracious and generous man who didn't offend tax collectors and prostitutes, but, on the other hand, he offended the religious elite. In other words, he was a man unconcerned with looking foolish before the most "important" people.

It is also disturbing just how often Jesus is seen sharing a table with those who question his authority and are seeking to destroy his ministry. To a degree this shouldn't surprise us. Those who lead often have their authority questioned. What is surprising is the way Jesus dealt with those who wanted to make him look bad. Read the Gospels, and it will shock you how many times Jesus goes into the houses of religious rulers and eats with them. This is disturbing too. Not because it is a bad practice, but because we know that Jesus is doing exactly what he said we should do: love our enemies. And if Jesus commanded us to do it and did it himself, then it must be something we should do as well. We know that, but we really don't want to do it because, well, we don't like our enemies. Loving our enemies looks weak. It feels like the first step in becoming what men are told to never be — well-trodden doormats.

Another reason men find Jesus frustrating is that he was willing to be vulnerable and weak. He had all the strength of God in him, yet he restrained himself and in full obedience submitted to God the Father. In his submission to God the Father, Jesus was willingly arrested and humiliated by the soldiers, stood silent before Pontius Pilate, and was deprived of any honor on the cross. The fully human, fully male Jesus conflicts with the ways we teach our boys to be men. We teach our boys that if they are real men, they won't let others disrespect them. But Jesus let people spit on him. We teach them that a man stands up for himself. But Jesus said nothing in his defense. We teach them to never back down and never go down without a fight. But Jesus chooses healing a man's ear instead of fighting. We teach them that real men are assertive. And yet, in the most defining moment of Jesus' life, the very reason he came, Jesus was passive as he allowed the decisions of others to dictate what would or would not happen to him.

This Jesus is difficult for men to relate to. This image of Jesus contradicts everything we are told men are to be, both by culture and by the church. We see a number of Christian books these days dedicated to helping men be "the warriors God created them to be," but very few books that exhort men to give up their authority so they can become servants. We hold up the whip-wielding Jesus for men to emulate, but very seldom do we point to the Jesus who weeps and cries out in deep emotion. We are quick to exhort men to be strong, but we rarely encourage men to embrace their weakness.

Fight Club Masculinity

In the opening scenes of the movie *Fight Club*, we find the narrator moving around his apartment, listlessly bemoaning what his life has been reduced to. While looking through an IKEA catalog, the narrator sighs and says, "Like so many others, I had become a slave to the IKEA nesting instinct." The opening scenes of the movie are a critique not just of the narrator's life but also of the marginalization of men in America. Masculinity, as portrayed in the movie, has been pushed to the edges of society and forced into an unnatural domestication such that men now care about décor. Society will not tolerate the aggressive, combative nature of men, and so men are driven underground to find an outlet for their frustration and a brotherhood they long for.

Enter Tyler Durden — the rescuer of the repressed male in *Fight Club*. Soon after the narrator meets Tyler, they go to a bar, where Tyler begins to attack the domestication of men.

"Do you know what a duvet is?... It's a blanket. Just a blanket. Now why do guys like you and I know what a duvet is? Is this essential to our survival? In the hunter-gatherer sense of the word? No. What are we then?... We're consumers. We're by-products of a lifestyle obsession."[8]

According to Tyler, in having left behind their calling to conquer the world, men have reduced themselves to consumers. It's no wonder men walk around like zombies; they have sold their souls for modern comforts. In the movie, Tyler and the narrator see a Calvin

Klein-esque ad on the side of a bus, and the narrator wonders, "Is that how a man looks like?"

To restore masculinity, Tyler creates fight clubs. Places where men can come together and feel alive. Where they can knock the shit out of other men and subversively push back against the feminization of a society in which men are crushed until they are no longer living. No longer human.

Before the beginning of the movie on the DVD, a quickly flashed warning appears, telling the viewer that living is exactly what is at stake.

> If you are reading this then this warning is for you. Every word you read of this useless fine print is another second off your life. Don't you have other things to do? Is your life so empty that you honestly can't think of a better way to spend these moments? Or are you so impressed with authority that you give respect and credence to all who claim it? Do you read everything you're supposed to read? Do you think everything you're supposed to think? Buy what you're told you should want? Get out of your apartment. Meet a member of the opposite sex. Stop the excessive shopping and masturbation. Quit your job. Start a fight. Prove you're alive. If you don't claim your humanity you will become a statistic. You have been warned ... Tyler[9]

The movie, with its message of reclaiming masculinity and providing space for male bonding, was so strong that fight clubs popped up all over the country. The warning from the beginning of the movie is something one could imagine hearing from provocative preachers around the country. Even churches and men's ministries wasted no time hopping on the "fight club" bandwagon, starting groups where men could be men and beat each other up. (They really exist. Google them.)

If you think it sounds odd for churches to start fight clubs and mixed martial arts groups, consider the fact that a nationally known pastor has been quoted in *Christianity Today* as saying things like this:

[Mark] Driscoll comes closest to imagining Jesus as the model of maleness when he argues that "latte-sipping Cabriolet drivers" do not represent biblical masculinity, because "real men"—like Jesus, Paul and John the Baptist—are "dudes; heterosexual, win-a-fight, punch-you-in-the-nose dudes." In other words, because Jesus is not a "limp-wristed, dress-wearing hippie," the men created in his image are not sissified church boys; they are aggressive, assertive, and nonverbal.[10]

Considering this, fight clubs in churches are a natural fit.

Muscular Christianity and *Fight Club* are sending the same message: Men are aggressive and made for combat. To stifle that is to stifle the very essence of a man.

Calling men to emulate a Tyler Durden-esque, punch-you-in-the-nose Jesus is simply exchanging one false image (the overly effeminate Jesus) for another. More than that, it seems utterly ridiculous when compared to the Sermon on the Mount. Muscular Christianity, which emphasizes the importance of morality, runs into a problem here. How does one align fighting or combat with the moral teachings of Jesus? Simple: Moral men don't start fights, but they do finish them. Throwing the first punch is seen as immoral and a lack of self-discipline. Throwing the second punch is redemptive and just. While this seems like wise discernment, it doesn't deal adequately with the words of Jesus when he says, "Blessed are the peacemakers," "If anyone slaps you on the right cheek, turn to them the other cheek also," and "Love your enemies and pray for those who persecute you."[11]

All-American Jesus

These hypermasculine portrayals of Jesus are readily embraced by American men. It may not be to the degree of a Tyler Durden, but the popularity of the Christian athlete is directly related to the muscular Christianity movement that spawned the YMCA and Fellowship of Christian Athletes. Using professional athletes to attract men to church has become a common practice. Not long ago, I went with a group of men from our church to a neighboring, larger church for the yearly kickoff event for their men's ministry. The place was packed with men, and you could tell the church wasn't quite ready for the turnout. Hundreds of men made time on a weeknight to come to a church function. I'll give you one guess as to why we from a neighboring church went to this event and why it was so well attended.

A star from the Indianapolis Colts was going to share his testimony.

Athletes have long been held up as prime examples of muscular Christians. They embody the spirit of the movement with their competitive, don't-back-down attitude and their testimony about Jesus. With their stories of discipline, competitiveness, hard work, and determination to pick themselves up and keep going after failure, they are an inspiration and reminder of what men are to strive for. In keeping with a celebrity-obsessed culture, athletes are perfect to help churches solve the mystery of getting men to attend.

After eating our meal of barbecue pork (did you expect anything different?), we filed into the main auditorium and waited for the program to begin as the volunteers scrambled to set up extra chairs for all the unexpected attendees.

And then the main show began. For slightly more than an hour, the pastor interviewed this well-known, well-loved football player about football, discipline, being a dad, and being a Christian. It wasn't horrible, and in places, I found it quite interesting. But honestly, I don't remember a thing he said. What I do remember is sitting there thinking to myself, *How many other men in this room could have done what he is doing right now? How many other stories would be just as powerful but will never be heard because they're not being told by an athlete?*

I'm not saying this particular athlete is bad — not at all. Nor am I saying we shouldn't hear the testimony of fellow believers. Just the opposite. But when we hold up the professional athlete as the premier Christian worth emulating, we are reinforcing both a culture of celebrity and a version of masculinity that most men are unable to attain.

Men may, in fact, be more inclined to combat and competition — with sword or pen or ball. Conflict, nonconformity, and resisting authority may well be a part of a man's nature. But just because these qualities are instinctual doesn't mean they are holy. As Sara Butler, a research associate at the Institute for American Values, writes, "If 'masculinity' is just a word for how men behave naturally, then the exhortation to 'be a man' loses all its power; it doesn't even make sense."[12]

As we said earlier, the fall of humanity touches every aspect of our being — including our most basic instincts. This is why following Jesus isn't about embracing what comes naturally to us; rather, it is about submitting all of ourselves to the cross of Christ so even our natural inclinations may die, thus rising with Christ in his resurrection so we may be made into a new creation. When Paul tells us that followers of Christ "have crucified the flesh,"[13] it includes all those dispositions, instincts, and inclinations that come prewired into the male gender. We are to crucify even that which is most natural to us, so all of who we are may be sanctified by the Holy Spirit. This is what muscular Christianity misses. It doesn't want testosterone chest thumping to die; it simply wants men to thump their chests for Jesus.

The Recovered Image

Jesus did not come to draw starker divisions between the genders. God did not send his Son into the world to encourage men to be more masculine or to rescue masculinity from the hands of women and liberals. Rather, Jesus, as the model for both men and women, calls all toward one singular end, namely, Christlikeness.

Men and women are to embody meekness, gentleness, self-control, and humility, as well as strength, courage, resolve, and boldness, as they grow in grace and in the knowledge of Jesus. This is what muscular Christianity distorts. A hypermasculine Jesus alienates both men and women from the real Jesus, who calls them to follow him. Humanity didn't need another dude; humanity needed a human, fully alive, to show us God's intended design. Through his relationship with God, interactions with others, and action in the world, Jesus shows what a human looks like when they are fully restored, sanctified, and freed from the brokenness brought about by sin. We discover that strength isn't defined by one's ability to bench-press, throw a football, or wield a sword, but in the quiet resolve to endure suffering as Christ suffered. Not backing down from conflict isn't a sign of strength. Bloodying your fists on the face of your enemy is not power. What Jesus demonstrated with his life is that strength is found when one's body, mind, and soul bear the scars that come from the gritty work of reconciliation.

What muscular Christianity got right was the impulse to attract men to the mission of God through the church. But what the movement got wrong was its bent toward creating hypermasculine caricatures of Jesus. These distortions are, at best, overly simplistic understandings of the man from Nazareth and, at worst, idols fashioned in our likeness. It portrayed Jesus as an All-American man rather than calling men to look like Jesus. Jesus is more complex and more human than we can imagine, which is why both men and women can grow into his likeness. Unfortunately, the movement started out too concerned with, and even in conflict with, what it perceived as a feminization of the church to recognize the equal call of men and women into the image of Christ. This anxious response incited a rejection of any characteristic that didn't fit the masculine stereotype it was propagating. In a sense, it rejected the fully human experience.

Men, the church needs us to fulfill its mission in the world, just as it needs women. Inclined toward action, we help keep the mission of the church moving forward. But we do not do this on our own. The mission of God moves forward when women and men taken action in the world alongside one another, not in conflict with each other.

If men are to fight, then we need to be clear what it is we fight for. Peace. Reconciliation. Grace. Justice. But let's be clear: We are made not for conflict but for action. There is a deep and profound difference here. Too often we equate not fighting with being a pushover, but one would have a hard time making the argument that "pushover" defines Jesus. Rather, we celebrate his quiet strength. This redefinition of strength forces us to reimagine how we take action in the world. So by all means, bloody your knuckles as you beat swords into plowshares. Show off your scars, but may they be scars you received from turning the other cheek. Men can even embrace competition in the gospel-sanctified way: "Outdo one another in showing honor."[14] Even defending truth, while looking like conflict, is about taking Christlike action in the world.

So, yes, Christianity should not create soft men. But neither should it create Christianized Tyler Durdens with oversized bravados. Men are attracted to a faith that is demanding and requires sacrifice. It isn't enough to just create activities that men enjoy; we need to ask men to die to themselves so that Christ might live in them. What if Christianity created men who look foolish, even weak, as we exchange a hypermasculine ideal for a more compassionate, empathetic, and human goal? What if we gave up our independence in exchange for dependence on Christ? What if we saw our dependence on Christ as a reason to be interdependent with each other? What if we found a reason to be sacrificially concerned with the cause of others? What if we found in Jesus permission to be fully authentic about our weakness and mistakes?

Maybe we would find the freedom to throw our heads back in laughter, just like in that picture in my office.

We might look like Jesus.

CHAPTER 5

JESUS

Well, I like the Christmas Jesus best and I'm saying grace.
When you say grace you can say it to grownup Jesus, or
teenage Jesus, or bearded Jesus or whoever you want.

Ricky Bobby

"Who do you say that I am?"

Jesus

If we want to know what it looks like to be a man, we look to Jesus. Which isn't as straightforward as it sounds.

I've never not known Jesus. I grew up in a Christian family whose parents and grandparents and aunts and uncles were faithful followers of Jesus. Our lives revolved around our faith, and our faith around being in church. Sunday wasn't just a day to go to church; it was a marathon of religious activity. Morning worship, Sunday school, family lunch, nap, youth group, and Sunday evening service were the major checkpoints of the day. Church activities went beyond Sunday and included Monday night Cadets (think Boy Scouts for Christians) and catechism classes on Wednesday night.

I have fond memories of all of this. I am grateful I have never not known Jesus. Sure, it isn't the sexiest testimony ever. Christians like the testimony of the person who lived a wretched life but one day woke up in a ditch after a drunken stupor to hear the voice of God saying, "I'm all you need," which leads them to come to Jesus and never touch alcohol again. We parade that person in front of church and clap and rejoice that God found this lost sinner and brought them home. And that's great and wonderful, and we *should* rejoice at that, but it causes some people to say, "Well, I don't really have a testimony" or "Mine's not that good." What? As a father, there is only one testimony I want my son to have — and it's the "I've never not known Jesus" one. We need to get better at celebrating that story.

Anyway . . .

From an early age, I knew all the stories of Jesus and the major doctrines of Christianity — including the life of Jesus and his imminent return. This got me thinking as a young kid. I don't remember exactly how old I was when I had this thought — maybe around the age of six — but I distinctly remember having it.

Jesus came as a child; Jesus is coming back; maybe Jesus will come back as a child ... maybe I'm Jesus!

Heresy can start at such a young age.

Had I told anyone this fanciful idea, my ego problems later in life might have been avoided.

While it seems like a ridiculous idea that should be expelled quickly from the mind of a kid, the more I've thought about it, the more I wonder, *Is it such a horrible thought?* To be clear, I'm not advocating heresy by saying we are Jesus, but rather, I'm wondering how differently I would live my life if I not only thought I was Jesus but lived as though I was.

How would I think differently?

How would I act differently?

How would I treat people?

How would I interact with those who hurt me?

How would I think about God?

How would I think about God's love for me?

I imagine there would be a significant difference in how I lived my life if I lived it as though I was Jesus.

As I write this, I am struck by the last question. So many people (myself included) think that God will love some future, perfected version of themselves. Until we become that perfected version, God simply tolerates us. He puts up with our constant failure around particular sins and is just waiting for us to prove ourselves, or else he'll pounce on us if we fail. But if I think about how God would love me if I was Jesus, I would simply say, "God loves me." Perfectly. Wholly. Completely. Which isn't horrible theology at all because the gospel is that Christ lived his life so that, in Jesus, we might become the righteousness of God.[1] Or, as many people like to say, God sees Jesus when he looks at us.

If God sees Jesus when he looks at us, maybe it's time to start acting like Jesus. Even, dare I say it, pretending to be Jesus.

Some may object to the idea of pretending to be Christ, but I didn't come up with this idea. In college, I was asked to speak at one of our weekly chapels, and at the time I was working my way through C. S. Lewis's *Mere Christianity*. It was there I first encountered the idea of pretending to be Jesus. Lewis wrote that when we pray the first words of the Lord's Prayer — *"Our Father"* — we are *"dressing up as Christ. If you like, you are pretending."*[2] Obviously, this is as outrageous as my son pretending he is a caracal (a bobcat-like animal that can jump eight to ten feet in the air; my son has my genes, so he cannot jump at all). So many of my actions fail to live up to even the pretense of being a son of God. Greed, jealousy, selfish ambition, and pervasive self-centeredness reveal how unlike Christ I am. And yet, when we examine Scripture, we see again and again that we are called to imitate, follow, dress up as, and generally be like Jesus as if we were Jesus.

- "Whoever claims to live in him must live as Jesus did." 1 John 2:6
- "In Christ Jesus you are all children of God through faith, for all of you who were baptized into Christ have clothed yourselves with Christ." Galatians 3:26 – 27
- "We all, who with unveiled faces contemplate the Lord's glory, are being transformed into his image with ever-increasing glory, which comes from the Lord, who is the Spirit." 2 Corinthians 3:18
- "Follow my example, as I follow the example of Christ." 1 Corinthians 11:1[3]
- "Follow God's example, therefore, as dearly loved children and walk in the way of love, just as Christ loved us and gave himself up for us as a fragrant offering and sacrifice to God." Ephesians 5:1 – 2

It seems that pretending to be Jesus isn't such a wacky idea but is actually a biblical idea. The reason we are told to imitate or dress up as Christ is simple: pretending to be like Jesus has a direct impact on how we think and act. Once again, let me quote C. S. Lewis:

Now, the moment you realise "Here I am, dressing up as Christ," it is extremely likely that you will see at once some way in which at that very moment the pretence could be made less of a pretence and more of a reality. You will find several things going on in your mind which would not be going on there if you were really a son of God. Well, stop them ...

You see what is happening. The Christ Himself, the Son of God who is man (just like you) and God (just like His Father) is actually at your side and is already at that moment beginning to turn your pretence into a reality.[4]

Central to the Christian life is the Spirit-led, disciplined work of sanctification moving us toward becoming like Jesus. This is what following Jesus is all about. Too many believe that Christianity exists to make us good, moral citizens. Christian Smith, in his important book *Soul Searching*, argues that Christianity in America is becoming a religion of Moralistic Therapeutic Deism.[5] Increasingly, it is believed that God exists to make us better persons, comfort us, and help us when we get into trouble while otherwise not interrupting our lives. The god of Moralistic Therapeutic Deism makes no requirement on the individual, no demand of sacrifice, but rather, is like a waiter in the sky who helps us get through life, making sure we get what we want.

This is not Jesus. Jesus makes real demands on our life. He calls us to take up our cross and follow him, dying to ourselves so he himself can live in us.[6] Jesus never says he will not burden us, only that his yoke is easy and his burden is light.[7] The end goal of Christianity is not to become a good, moral person. Don't get me wrong, morality is part of holiness, so yes, following Jesus will lead us toward being moral. But that is not the point of following Jesus. We follow Jesus to become like Jesus.

Jesus, then, becomes our focus. He defines reality, how we should live, and what we should do. Our lives are no longer defined by culture around us but by Christ. Jesus becomes the filter through which we see and understand ourselves, others, and the world. Our world, whether we see it or not, is shaped and sustained by and dripping with the very presence of Christ.[8] And so we need to remove the filters of culture and self and expectations and replace them with the filters of Christ to see the world. Jesus models, explains, and clarifies not just what we see but what we should see in ourselves, in others, and in the world.

So if we want to know what it means to be a son or daughter of God, we look to Jesus. If we want to know what it means to be perfect, we look to Jesus. If we want to know what it means to love others, we look to Jesus. If we want to know what it means to be human, we look to Jesus.

That's what is missing from so many of our definitions of masculinity. They are not focused on the new man, Jesus. Too many definitions are based on a James Bond, George Washington, or John Wayne ideal that has been impressed on men through media. Jesus, as the one perfect person who fully embodied what it meant to be human and is the new Adam, is the definition of what it means to be a man. Everything else is false.

The Humble Servant

In the Gospels, we often see the disciples arguing about who is the greatest among them. Which is, after all, what all people do. Get a group of people together, and a pecking order begins to emerge. That person is the leader; the one over there is the organizer; this one is the butt of all jokes. It just happens. So it shouldn't surprise us or make us think less of the disciples for engaging in that exercise.

Piecing the story together from the gospels of both Luke and John, we see that, at the Last Supper, a dispute broke out between the disciples about who was the greatest among them. Luke says it happened after Jesus broke the bread and blessed the cup. John doesn't say anything about the bread and cup, only that the meal was served and that Jesus "got up from the meal, took off his outer clothing, and wrapped a towel around his waist. After that, he poured water into a basin and began to wash his disciples' feet, drying them with the towel that was wrapped around him."[9]

I don't know if it actually happened this way, but I want to believe the following is exactly how it went down:

Jesus and his disciples gathered in the upper room. Jesus knew this was the last time he would dine with his closest friends, but they were unaware of what lay ahead. As the meal was served, Jesus took his place at the table and reached for some bread. He quietly lifted the bread into the air, gave thanks, and then spoke these words: "This is my body, given for you. As often as you eat this bread, do so in remembrance of me." Slowly, he set the bread down. There was a quiet reverence about him that mystified the unaware disciples and gave rise to their silence. Jesus grasped the cup, again gave thanks, and lifted it into the air, saying, "This is the new covenant in my blood. As often as you drink this cup, do so in remembrance of me."

To the disciples this was strange. Jesus had been cryptic lately, but this was especially odd. But the meal went on, and conversation went as conversation goes. It wasn't long before the disciples revisited a debate they had had before: *Who among us is the greatest?* This conversation isn't unique to the disciples but is one that many men have had over many years. Men are constantly sizing each other up. Eyeing the room as they wonder who they can take. Who is the smartest? Who is the strongest? Who is the leader, and who is the leader when the leader is gone? Is it me?

As the volume increased in the room, Jesus, without a word, got up from the table. One of the disciples shouted his qualifications for being at Jesus' right hand when Jesus entered his glory. Jesus took off his outer garment. Laughter filled the room as one disciple pointed out the failure of another in being a man. Jesus knelt down and took a foot of the nearest disciple and began to wash it.

And everything went silent.

Because the greatest was willing to be the least.

Washing feet was reserved for the person at the bottom of the pecking order. It was the task for the lowliest of the lowly. Peers did not wash each other's feet. In fact, some thought it was wrong for a Jewish slave to wash the feet of another Jew, so they would assign a Gentile slave to do the task. And here was Jesus, the Messiah, voluntarily on his knees to wash the dirt and grime off his disciples' feet.

Imitating Christ means imitating his humility. Not just an "aw, shucks" humility, but a willingness to be seen as less than you are. To relinquish one's rights to privilege, honor, and service for the sake of another. Jesus reveals this to be the true mark of a man. Of a human.

Closely related to this is the idea of *kenosis*—or emptying oneself—found in Paul's letter to the Philippians in one of the most breathtaking descriptions of Jesus in the New Testament, the one "who, being in very nature God, did not consider equality with God something to be used to his own advantage; rather, he made himself nothing by taking the very nature of a servant, being made in human likeness."[10]

Jesus, in becoming human, emptied himself. This does not mean Jesus emptied himself of his divinity. Quite the contrary. But to be fully human, Jesus needed to subject his divine prerogative to the limitations of humanity. Thus we see Jesus limited in things like knowing when he will return and being able to do only what he sees the Father doing.

What would it look like for men to willingly empty themselves? To give up their position to another? To stop requiring other men to prove themselves? For husbands to serve their wives in a relationship of mutual submission?

What would it look like if men were to become the greatest

servants the world has ever known, willing to sacrifice all that they have as they imitate the love of Jesus for others?

Men don't need to learn how to fight, how to be wild, or how to kill a bear to become manlier. Holding Jesus as our example, we see that men need to learn how to be humble and serve others. And honestly, imitating the humility of Christ, being willing to be seen as a lesser man in the eyes of others, takes an incredible amount of courage.

Revelation Manhood

Of course, some will resist the humble servant portrait of Jesus, quickly pointing to the more macho descriptions of Jesus. The first of these is found in Revelation.

No book in the Bible is more debated and mysterious than the book of Revelation. It is a complicated book filled with metaphors and images that have sparked controversy and a vast array of interpretations. I remember staying up late at night as a teenager reading Revelation, trying to make sense of it, convinced I could crack the code. I can't tell you how many Bible studies I've been a part of that have studied Revelation. In all my reading and studying and conversation, I think I have finally figured out Revelation: Jesus wins. That's the point. Everything else is conjecture.

John's portrayal of Jesus in Revelation depicts a wildly different Jesus than the one revealed in the Gospels, where Jesus is seen teaching, preaching, healing, suffering, dying, and resurrecting. Jesus is not even portrayed as a human male in the book.[11] Instead, we see Jesus as an angel, a lamb, and a warrior with eyes "like blazing fire."[12] Moving in and out of the scenes of Revelation with ease, Jesus shows up in astonishing forms when least expected. We see him worthy to open the scroll, magnificent enough to cause all creation to worship him, valiant enough to slay the beast, and loving enough to welcome his bride.

This is the Jesus we worship, and there is little question as to why. We worship the glorified Christ of Revelation 19, but we do not imitate him. Our model for behavior as humans is not the postresurrection, exalted Christ, but the incarnate Jesus who walked the earth and got dust on his feet and suffered. This is why Paul wanted to share in Christ's sufferings. He knew that imitating Christ began with imitating how he suffered. It is only when "we share in his sufferings" that we "also share in his glory."[13]

But let's be real: If ever there was a Jesus "real men" would want to imitate, it is the stallion-riding, eyes-blazing, sword-swinging warrior Jesus of Revelation 19. On the surface, it seems like this is a Jesus we can relate to. One who looks like we want to look. But, let's look again, because what we see may surprise us.

John looks up, and the heavens open to reveal Jesus on a white horse, waging war to provide justice. His head is adorned with many crowns; the armies of heaven are following him; and he is dressed in a robe dipped in blood. Referencing this portrayal of Jesus, one prominent pastor said, "Jesus is a pride fighter with a tattoo down his leg, a sword in His hand, and the commitment to make someone bleed."[14] This is not only a Jesus men can imitate but, we are told, a man they *should* imitate.

However, a closer look reveals that the rider's robe, as described in verse 13, has been dipped in blood before Jesus even encounters his enemies. This has led many to argue that the blood on the robe is not the blood of Jesus' enemies but is his own blood. One commentary on Revelation states, "In the Apocalypse, Christ conquers not by shedding the blood of his enemies, but by shedding his blood *for his enemies*."[15] People often point to Revelation 19 and say, "See! Jesus wasn't a pansy. He wasn't some peace-loving hippy who never fought. He is a warrior, not afraid to get in there and shed some blood!"

True, Jesus is not a pansy, is not meek and mild, and is not a doormat. But Jesus wasn't a warrior in the typical sense. He didn't

JESUS

fight with brute might, brandishing a sword to draw blood from his enemies. In fact, the sword in Revelation 19 is double-edged and comes out of his mouth. Sound familiar? Jesus fights with the authority of his word, not with his biceps. More than that, Jesus fights by giving himself. Jesus fights his enemies with the love he has for them as evidenced by the cross. And this love for his enemies includes his love for you and me. In his letter to the Colossians, Paul writes, "Once you were alienated from God and were enemies [of God] in your minds."[16] It was then that Jesus died for us.

Jesus does make someone bleed, but it isn't his enemies. *He* bleeds.

This is consistent with what we see earlier in Revelation. John hears an angel cry out, "Who is worthy to break the seals and open the scroll?"[17] John weeps because no one is found worthy. One of the elders speaks up and tells John there is one, though, who is worthy. In walks, not a warrior, not a lion, not a bicep-bulging beast of a man, but "a Lamb, looking as if it had been slain."[18] Jesus, the Lamb, is worthy because he has been slain.

Imitating Jesus begins when we are willing to be slain. Willing to be raked over the coals. Willing to be seen as weak. Very few men will say, "I want to be known as a lamb." But what does it say that Jesus was willing to be seen as a lamb? It seems he is redefining not only masculinity but strength as well. Jesus reveals that what we think is weak is actually strong. If we were to define masculinity by this Jesus, we would have to admit that masculine strength is not the ability to defeat one's enemies with a show of raw power, but masculine strength that imitates the actions of Jesus is the willingness to lay down one's life for another—including for the lives of one's enemies.

In a culture where men defend their honor, where they do not display weakness, where they are told to "grow some balls" the actions of Jesus are ludicrous. We're not supposed to back down from our enemies. We don't let them walk over us. We don't go down without a fight. But Jesus inverts all of that and shows us that the way we're to fight evil is not with fists but with outstretched arms of love.

How different might masculinity look if it were modeled after the Lamb who was slain?

Wielding the Whip

I don't know this for a fact, but my guess is that Indiana Jones did more for the sale of whips in the 1980s than anybody else. I learned to crack a whip because of those movies. In Indiana's hands, the whip wasn't just a weapon. He used it to swing from one place to another; grab his father, who was on a conveyor of sorts; latch on to a truck as he slid underneath it; and, of course, rope a girl. In an age of guns, Indiana's reliance on such a simple weapon sparked my imagination.

The same can be said of the whip-wielding Jesus who clears the temple. Christians have long used this passage as justification for Christian violence. John Calvin, who has been influential in my life, disappointingly used the whip-wielding Jesus to justify the execution of Michael Servetus.[19] The death penalty, just war, punishment of schismatics, and killing of heretics have all been defended by pointing to the whip-in-hand Jesus.

Not only is this passage often referenced in relationship to violence, but to masculinity as well.[20] Those who bemoan the feminization of the church hold up Jesus wielding a whip as an image of what it would mean to recapture a masculine Christianity. In the temple we see a forceful Jesus. A Jesus who stands up for what is right. We see Jesus, in righteous anger, clearly outlining what is proper behavior in the Father's house — someone not opposed to getting his hands dirty to defend truth.

Our culture celebrates this Jesus, but some in the ancient Roman culture interpreted the indignant anger of Jesus in the temple as an effeminate characteristic.[21] In fact, Marcus Aurelius, the emperor-philosopher, wrote, "In moments of anger, let the thought always be present that loss of temper is no sign of manliness, but that there is more virility, as well as more natural humanity, in one who shows himself gentle and peaceable ... Anger is as much a mark of weakness as is grief; in both of them men receive a wound and submit to a defeat."[22] One's tendency to be overcome with anger was a sign that one was not yet a man in the eyes of many Romans.

But Jesus redefines the Roman understanding of masculinity and anger by showing us what righteous anger looks like. Jesus didn't explode in an uncontrollable rage; his anger was controlled and carefully calculated.

Weapons were not allowed in the temple area. Jesus did not bring a whip into the temple, but after he saw what was taking place in the outer court, he began to burn with anger. John's gospel tells us that he "made a whip out of cords."[23] Because he was already inside the temple court, Jesus had to use materials available there. Likely, this would have been straw and fodder from animals' stalls or perhaps a rope used to tie up an animal.[24] It would not have been made of leather, like Indiana Jones's, or studded with rocks and metal, like the whips of the Romans. We're talking a reed-like whip strong enough to move cattle, and that's about it. Overturning the tables wasn't meant to harm the merchants, but to disrupt their business. The actions of Jesus in the temple were carried out with a lot of thought, but they weren't the violent, aggressive, fear-inducing acts that some would have us believe.

While using this passage to argue for acts of violence is questionable, it is clear that imitating Jesus requires us to be willing to take a stand for what is right, good, beautiful, and truthful. In some circumstances, it is appropriate to let righteous anger drive our actions. But we should not be overcome by anger and lose our ability to evaluate and control our actions. Christians are never commanded to avoid anger, rather we are told to not sin in our anger.[25] Anger that is rooted in dismay at truth that is pushed aside, at injustice, at instances of people being marginalized, at situations of abuse, or at the gospel being defamed can lead a person to take a stand for truth—even if it is unpopular.

Clearing the temple of the money changers and merchants was an act of conviction that men should emulate—as should women as well. Men and women should both commit to defending truth, the gospel, and the cause of the oppressed. Categorizing the actions of Jesus in the temple as masculine unnecessarily alienates women from the call to take a stand for truth.

Nowhere does the Bible say that Jesus came to model masculinity. Rather, in his letter to the Colossians, Paul writes that Jesus is "the firstborn over all creation."[26] This means Jesus is the new model for both men and women, and in him, men and women are brought together as they seek to imitate Christ.

Imitating Jesus is not a call issued exclusively to men. Jesus did not come to restore masculinity, but rather, God incarnated himself in Jesus to restore humanity—both men and women. Women are to imitate Christ as much as men are—including the image of a whip-wielding Jesus who takes an ardent stand for truth. Even those who advocate more conservative gender roles acknowledge that "masculinity is by no means the exclusive domain of men."[27] In other words, some of what we deem "masculine" is simply referring to characteristics associated with the male gender, but in reality these characteristics are something both men and women should strive for. When characteristics are godly, they transcend masculinity and femininity and become traits that all people should seek to embody.

What we also see in this story is that the anger of Jesus over the misuse of the temple was deeply rooted in a growing sadness over the spiritual condition of his fellow Jews. As manly as Jesus was in the temple, the sadness he felt was expressed in less-than-manly ways. In

Luke 13, we see Jesus approaching Jerusalem and in a moment of sorrow expressing a maternal desire to "gather your children together, as a hen gathers her chicks under her wings."[28] Then, in chapter 19, Jesus triumphantly enters the city of Jerusalem on the back of a donkey. The people are shouting, "Blessed is the king who comes in the name of the Lord!" As he approaches, Jesus begins weeping over the city.[29]

Both of these instances are more aligned with feminine characteristics than masculine ones. Weeping and referring to himself as a mother hen? When was the last time you heard a male cheerfully referring to himself as a chicken? We are more familiar with the opposite—men working hard to prove themselves *not* a chicken, lest they look feminine.

In Jesus, both feminine and masculine characteristics are present and influence his actions.

It's Complex

Any effort to pigeonhole Jesus as a bicep-bulging prize fighter sporting tattoos neglects the less than macho actions of Jesus and the feminine characteristics he embodies. Recasting Jesus as the ultimate manly man is simply an overly anxious response to a concern that "Jesus the man" is being co-opted by an overly feminine caricature, thus making him meek and mild and a turnoff to men. However, if cultural expectations of men are simply imposed on Jesus because we think he has been portrayed as too feminine, we make Jesus into our image and invert the caricature. The radical nature of his humanity is lost as we force Jesus to reflect our cultural ideals of masculinity rather than understanding and defining those ideals through him. The redemption of masculinity in Jesus begins when we accept Jesus as the man he was, not as the man we want him to be—we let him cry and comfort and nurture as he stands for truth and rebukes and disciplines.

If Jesus looks too feminine to us, maybe it says more about our understanding of masculinity than it does about a possible conspiracy to feminize the church and men.

To understand the masculinity Jesus embodied, we must submit our perceptions, expectations, and even comforts to what we find in Scripture. There we find a masculinity that rebuked Pharisees and stood up for truth. That was willing to sacrifice himself, not just for those he loves, but for his enemies as well. A man who was willing to assume the role of a servant. A man who was unashamed to show emotion and shed tears.

Saying Jesus defines what it means to be a man is easy; actually defining manhood in light of Jesus is harder. Because which Jesus do we define men by? The warrior Jesus of Revelation 19 who fights his enemies by being willing to suffer at their hands? The servant Jesus who kneels down to wash feet? The whip-wielding Jesus who stands for truth and clears the temple? What about the Jesus who likens himself to a mother hen and weeps unashamedly over Jerusalem? Do we define masculinity by all of these? In a word—yes. Which makes defining manhood, according to Jesus, ridiculously complex.

Which might be the point.

CHAPTER 6

DELIGHTING IN WEAKNESS

Shame is the most powerful, master emotion. It's the fear that we're not good enough.

Brené Brown

There is a time in a boy's life when the sweetness is pounded out of him; and tenderness, and the ability to show what he feels, is gone.

Norah Vincent

I've always been an emotional guy. To give you an example of how emotional I am, I once cried during *Tommy Boy*. You know, the Chris Farley movie where he plays an idiot (every Chris Farley movie) opposite David Spade (half of Chris Farley's movies) trying to save the family business. In the scene following the death of his father, Tommy is walking down a country road, autumn leaves blowing in the wind and mournful music playing as he grieves. Seeing him all alone on the road after his dad had died made me think about my dad and how I would feel if he died unexpectedly.

I'm watching a Chris Farley movie, and I'm crying.

I think it's safe to say that anyone who cries during *Tommy Boy* is a wee bit emotional.

That doesn't mean I have always been comfortable with emotions. When we were first married, my wife would come home from her job as a special education teacher and tell me about her day. On bad days, after I'd listen to her stories about kids who were hard to work with or about dealing with some "politics" among the teachers, I would offer advice on how to fix whatever situation was bothering her. At one point, she looked at me and adamantly said, "I don't need you to fix this; I just need you to empathize with me!"

But empathizing with her meant I would have to understand my emotions so I could understand hers, and I wasn't interested in understanding my emotions. I wasn't even interested in feeling my emotions. I think I was like most men, who see emotions as not something to be felt but something to be fixed. Fixing emotions, or addressing the situation that is causing unwanted emotions, is a way in which men distance themselves from what they are feeling. If I can fix the situation, or can at least pour myself into working to fix the situation, then I can ignore my feelings. Ignoring my emotions was how I dealt with them. I didn't want to feel them. I wouldn't let myself feel them. I learned through multiple experiences that the display of emotions wasn't safe. Crying in school. Telling a girl how I felt about her. Asking other boys to quit calling me names because they were hurting my feelings. Shame is a powerful teacher, and it had taught me that emotions were not my friend; they were instead a sign of being weak. And men are not weak.

Pounding Weakness into Me

Middle school was an absolutely horrific time in my life. Its explosive concoction of hormones, social unrest, and awkwardness make it ideal for tormenting nearly everyone who walks the halls of the school.

The first week of seventh grade is forever etched in my memory because it established my social standing for the rest of middle school. It was first period in the morning, and we were in English class. I was seated near the front of the class, and one of my friends from elementary school, Brian, was in the next row over, and just a couple seats behind me. The class had been given a short assignment, and both Brian and I finished early. We used the time before the teacher started teaching again to engage in the wonderfully edifying game of calling each other insulting names.

Don't ask. I have no idea why. I can only assume it was because we were cool, mature seventh graders.

It wasn't mean-spirited, but it was competitive. I don't remember a single name I called Brian, and I can only remember one name he called me. I remember it because it became my name for all of middle school.

Pillsbury Doughboy.

Pills. Doughboy. Pillsbury. Pick your iteration, this is what I was called for the rest of my middle school career. This name was a shame-filled dark cloud that followed me around every day. I couldn't get away from the name. Nothing I did removed it. Ignoring it, rolling with it, laughing about it, fighting it—nothing mattered. Society had spoken, and this was who I was in their eyes. It is amazing how deep that name cut. For as much as I tried to brush it off, "Pillsbury" had become such a deep place of shame for me that, even to this day, I hate telling people about this nickname. Hate it. I even considered not including the story in this book because of how deep this wound is for me. Pillsbury Doughboy represents everything that is out of my control. It was something I couldn't change. Something chosen by others to define me. No matter how much I tried, no matter what I did, that name became a constant reminder that I was not good enough, not powerful enough, not in control enough to change my reality. Every time someone called out, "Pillsbury," I was reminded of this simple truth: I am weak.

No one ever told me this outright, but I learned it quickly enough: Men are not weak. All boys learn it, and all men know it. If you want to be a man, you cannot be weak. It doesn't matter if it is emotionally weak or mentally weak or physically weak; to be a man is to be strong.

So I worked hard to become strong. It started with being mentally strong. I began telling myself I was better than everyone else. School was always easy for me, and I was placed in advanced math and science classes early on. This made it easy to prove I was, in fact, better than others. I was smarter than them. In class, people wanted to be near me to get help and ask to copy off my papers. No, I didn't just give them the answers and let them copy off me. Giving them the answers would give up my social leverage. If you wanted to get answers, you had to give something. Intelligence, for me, became a source of strength. A source of pride. In my head, it became a shield that protected me. "Call me all the names you want, but in the end, I am stronger than you."

In high school I began lifting weights—something I do to this day. Body image became—and honestly still is—very important to me. The Pillsbury Doughboy is soft and flabby, and someone is constantly jabbing a finger into his midsection. So I worked at becoming hard. I hoped that if I made my body hard and strong, it would be so different from the image of the Doughboy that it wouldn't make any sense to call me Pillsbury.

And it worked.

I remember a time in tenth grade when a group of guys were talking in the hallway before school, and someone called me Doughboy. I remember my face flushing because it had been a long time since someone called me "the name," and the fear of it catching on caused my stomach to sink. As my mind raced while I tried to figure out how to respond, someone in the group said, "I don't think we can call him that anymore because he's lost all his baby fat."

Not exactly what I was looking for, but I took it.

Being the Pillsbury Doughboy taught me a common (but utterly debilitating) lesson about being a man: You cannot be weak. Perceived weakness will not be tolerated by other men. Any weakness present in a man will be brought to the surface to be ridiculed and shamed away. Weakness must be covered over with bravado and T-shirts that proclaim "pain is just weakness leaving the body," perpetuating the ever popular myth that we can and should eradicate weakness.

So I learned to be strong and to exude strength. I hid my emotions from people so I wouldn't look weak. I pretended the insults weren't the sticks and stones that wounded my heart, but that they were mere words bouncing off my rubber exterior. Being strong, I believed, is what I needed to do to protect myself. Being strong was being a man.

Breaking Out of the Box

At some point in their lives, most men are told that being weak is unacceptable for a man. They must "man up," "soldier on," and "be strong." There is a degree in which the exhortation to be strong is appropriate. I look at my son and think about him growing up and going to school, and I do not want him to grow up weak. I want him to be strong in all areas of his life—physically, mentally, spiritually, and emotionally. I want him to be strong enough to stand up to bullies, strong enough to stand by his convictions, and strong enough to stand with the outcast. He, like all of us, needs to learn that he is stronger than he thinks he is.

And yet, as much as I want him to be strong, I also know there will be times when he will be weak. He will be overpowered by life. Use all his strength to stand against what is uncontrollable, only to be left feeling weak and inadequate.

But the moment a man shows weakness his masculinity comes into question. Men are not allowed to be weak.

In her book *Daring Greatly*, Brené Brown recounts the story of a young man who demonstrated what it was like to live under the weight of having to hide his weakness from others. This man, who was well over six feet tall, stood up and said, " 'Imagine living like this,' as he crouched down and pretended that he was stuffed inside a small box. Still hunched over, he said, 'You really only have three choices. You spend your life fighting to get out, throwing punches at the side of the box and hoping it will break. You always feel angry and you're always swinging. Or you just give up. You don't give a shit about anything.' At that point he slumped over on the ground."[1]

This is the experience of more men than we can count. This is my experience. We as men are caught in an irreconcilable double standard where we are told to be vulnerable and show our weaknesses, only to have the snot beat out of us when we do.

Here's the dirty secret, though: If men are unable to be weak, they will be unable to be vulnerable. And if they are unable to be vulnerable, their relationships will lack intimacy. And if their relationships lack intimacy, men will suffer from chronic loneliness.

Remember back to the first chapter, where I wrote of being at a leadership retreat in Houston. I had told Jim I was feeling lonely, like no one really knew me. It has taken me a while to fully understand what I really meant by that. Up to that point in my life, I believed I was liked, respected, and good friends with people. I wasn't some sort of recluse who lived in a cave. For the most part, I was seen as one of those people who was accepted by most social groups. So even though I felt lonely, I wasn't sure why. What I have come to see is that while I was friends with a lot of people, I wasn't really known by any of them. They knew the image I had crafted. The one I wanted them to know. But they didn't know me. The result was that I felt separated, cut off, isolated from nearly everyone because I didn't dare to be vulnerable and expose all of who I was, including my fears, failures, and weaknesses.

The constant pressure to be strong causes many men to ignore their emotions. Emotions that display weakness — vulnerability, dependence, compassion, insecurity, joy, tenderness — are replaced by a strong, hypermasculine, unemotional pose. There are really only two emotions that are socially acceptable for a man to exhibit: anger and jealousy, and of these two, anger has become the dominant, go-to emotion for men. So rather than feeling afraid, men feel angry. Rather than feeling sad, men feel angry. Rather than feeling hurt, men feel angry. Rather than feeling crushed, men feel angry. Rather than feeling helpless, men feel angry. You get the point, and you can probably see the truth of this by simply observing how angry young boys and men are these days. It is no wonder men are primarily responsible for violent behavior — homicide, road rage, school shootings, blowing up buildings, domestic violence, racism, and bullying.[2]

I have discipled many guys, and we'll often have a conversation at some point where they'll tell me about something that happened to them. Some experience in their past that wounded them. In the course of our conversation, I'll typically ask them how that experience made them feel. Almost every time I ask, the first response I get begins something like, "I just need to ..." or "Next time I'll ..." or "I wish I would have ..." Rather than telling me how the experience made them feel, they tell me what they're going to do to not feel again whatever it is they felt. I have to keep digging to get them to share how they feel. The myth here is that they can't tell me how they feel because men don't feel emotions. Anyone who says that should make sure their pants are not on fire. Men, like women, are full of emotion. The difference is that women are told their emotions are natural and it's okay for them to feel and talk about them. Men are told they shouldn't have emotions, and if they do, they should hide them so they don't look like women. Because we don't want our men to appear weak, we fail to teach them how to be emotionally intelligent, thus leaving boys and men to a solitary struggle of hiding their emotions. In their book *Raising Cain*, Dan Kindlon and Michael Thompson acknowledge this fact about our culture: "[It] supports emotional development for girls and discourages it for boys."[3] Boys are taught to steer clear of their emotions and hide their feelings and fears so as to not appear feminine. Thus, boys grow into men who have limited emotional intelligence. In a world of uncertainty where a toolbox of emotions is needed to navigate complex interpersonal relationships, men have a hammer. Rather than appearing weak by expressing fears, anxiety, and sadness, boys and men turn to aggression and anger. Is it any wonder that violence in schools has escalated? Our boys do not have the emotional intelligence necessary to navigate the world and "need an emotional vocabulary that expands their ability to express themselves in ways other than anger or aggression."[4]

Men, if we want to be healthy, we have to learn how to be present to our emotions and courageous enough to be vulnerable and expose them to others. Women, if you want your husband, friends, or sons to be healthy, you have to allow them space to be vulnerable, and when they are, you must avoid looking at them as less than men. Women say they want their men to be vulnerable, but many men experience rejection from women when they *are* vulnerable. Men will only learn to be vulnerable when they have a safe place free of judgment and condemnation.

The Power of Vulnerability

We hide our emotions because we believe they make us look weak, and our culture tells us men cannot be weak. However, the Bible encourages an understanding of masculinity that leads both to being vulnerable and delighting in weakness.

In his second letter to the Corinthians, Paul tells us he learned to "delight in weakness," saying, "When I am weak, then I am strong."[5] Weakness, for Paul, is not something to be ashamed of but to embrace to see the power of Christ work in and through a person. If we never learn to be weak, we will never learn to rely on the power of God. Culture says we need to find the inner strength that's ours simply because we are men. The Bible tells us we need to abandon our own strength and see how weak we truly are, so we may learn to depend on Christ's strength.

There are going to be times in our lives when we are not strong enough to change the situation. Cancer. The loss of a job because of an economic crisis. Losing a loved one in a car accident. Only when we realize how truly little control we have over the world around us will we begin to accept just how weak we are. And if we can embrace our weakness in the world and stop the pretense that we are super-natural he-men impervious to the threats of a broken world, then we will begin to see the strength of Christ move in and through us.

The Bible, once again, inverts the cultural mandate placed on men.

Accepting our weakness begins by allowing ourselves to be vulnerable. The dictionary defines vulnerability as "capable of being physically and emotionally wounded; open to attack or damage." That's every man I know. Not every man will admit it, but every man is. If a guy goes up to a woman and asks her for a date, he is being vulnerable and opening himself up to emotional wounding and rejection. If a man courageously stands up for what is right at work, he runs the risk of being fired.

Men don't always feel it's acceptable to be vulnerable. Men often battle a double standard where they're asked to be strong and courageous and run toward risk, while at the same time they're told they are weak if they admit to being hurt or scared. The result is that neither weakness nor vulnerability is attractive to men. But if you want to follow Jesus and live the way he calls you to live, you must take the posture of someone who is open to being wounded.

We readily accept the man who vulnerably risks his life. We just call it courage. David was amazingly vulnerable as he stood before Goliath with only a sling. Unfortunately, we don't think of emotional vulnerability in the same way. We see it as weak, not courageous. But when we are courageously vulnerable with our emotions, it has a dramatic impact.

In 2013, my wife and I found out we were pregnant. Getting pregnant with our first child was difficult, and the second was proving to be just as difficult. So when my wife told me about the positive test result, I was ecstatic. But her face didn't look as joyful as mine felt. "It just feels different. Like something isn't right." Always the optimist, I told her not to worry until after we had been to the doctor. Tests were done, and once they had been analyzed, the doctor came into the room and sat down. His face proved my wife right. The pregnancy was ectopic, meaning the egg had implanted in the fallopian tubes rather than in the womb. The pregnancy would have to be terminated.

We were crushed.

A few days later, I asked my wife if I could write a blog post about what happened and what I was feeling. She agreed. I wrote. It was the most vulnerable post I had ever done. I didn't try to hide the fact that we were hurting, or pretend that we were doing okay. I wrote of our pain. Our confusion. Our need for something more than cliché Christian sayings. I wrote about hope.

I posted the blog at 10:45 p.m. Not the optimum time to post a blog. By morning it had received nearly fifteen hundred views, which for me at the time was a great post.

By the end of the day, it was nearly five thousand.

By the end of the next day, nearly twenty thousand.

To date this post has more than two and a half million views.

What is more amazing is the response I've gotten. Comments, emails, notes, Facebook messages — all from people who found hope because someone had the courage to be vulnerable.

Vulnerability has the power to change us and those around us if we are courageous enough. Running into a burning building requires courage. So does sharing our story. Our vulnerability gives people permission to be vulnerable. Nowhere is this clearer than in how Jesus lived his life. And this courageous vulnerability is how Jesus depicted God's love for humanity.

The parable of the prodigal son reveals the heart of God the Father as much as, if not more than, any other passage of Scripture.[6] Calling the story "The Prodigal Son" focuses our attention on the son. We have to get beyond the well-known title an editor gave the story to see it is about more than just the son, or even the two sons; it is actually about the Father. A far better title, in my opinion, is "The Loving Father" or maybe even "The Vulnerable Father."

Kenneth Bailey, in his book *Poet and Peasant*, helped me see this story in a new light.[7] The unfettered love of the father is seen at the very beginning of the story when the son asks the father for his inheritance. Many who have heard this story preached in church probably know this request was akin to saying, "Dad, I wish you would hurry up and die so I can have my inheritance." What is most shocking about this request is that the father actually grants it.

For starters, in a highly patriarchal society in which the father is sovereign, the son is lucky he didn't get a beating. Really lucky. Second, wealth wasn't measured in dollars and cents, like it is now, but was wrapped up in assets. The inheritance the son received would come in the form of land and animals. But according to Bailey, if the son wanted to sell it, even if the inheritance had already been divided up, the father had to give the son the right to dispose of the wealth — which he obviously has done, because the son is able to take his inheritance to a distant country. Nobody is traveling to a far-off country with a plot of land in their back pocket, let alone a herd of sheep.

What is more, the inheritance the father gives to the son is actually the father's retirement money. As the father got older, he would live off his land as his sons worked it. So by allowing the son to dispose of his inheritance, the father is putting his own future in jeopardy. He is becoming economically vulnerable on behalf of the son.

One more thing on the giving of the inheritance: For the giving of the inheritance to be considered legal, the father could not give it to the son under duress — including emotional duress. If asked, the father must say he gave his son the inheritance as a gift.

We are told the ungrateful son squanders all his wealth and decides it would be better to go home and ask his father to hire him as a servant. The son prepares a speech and heads home, practicing his speech the whole way. Meanwhile, the father has been scanning the horizon every day, watching for the son's return.

We should note that when the son told his father to drop dead and then sold his family's property, he wasn't giving the finger just to his family but to his community as well. Not to mention the fact that when he left his family, he went to a distant country—likely a Gentile country—and ended up working with pigs—something a good Jewish person would never consider doing. In other words, this Jewish son left his family, his community, and his faith. If the son were ever to return home, the community would berate him. He probably wouldn't even make it into town before a mob formed to mock, ridicule, and taunt the son in hopes of shaming him into running away again.

Back to the story. Every morning, the father gets up and goes out to watch the road coming into town, hoping his son will return home. And then he sees him. The father knows the humiliation that is waiting for his son when he gets to town, so the father, gathering up his robe in his hands, takes off running toward his son!

In those days, well-to-do men in robes didn't run, because it was considered a disgrace. By running toward his son, the father is opening himself up to humiliation. He will be mocked by the community. The community, which would have mocked the son, can no longer mock the son, because the father is willing to make a spectacle of himself, humiliating himself in front of the community on behalf of the son.

The father runs up to his son, and just as the son begins his speech, the father lavishes him with kisses. In that moment, all the son can do is give part of his speech. His whole speech was, "I have sinned against heaven and against you. I am no longer worthy to be called your son; make me like one of your hired servants." It was a halfhearted effort to keep his pride. But all he can get out while his father is kissing him is, "I have sinned against heaven and against you. I am no longer worthy to be called your son." I don't know why, but perhaps it is the kindness of the father that changed the heart of the son. I want to believe that, as the son saw his father running, making a scene and humiliating himself on his behalf, his heart melted in response to the loving-kindness of his dad.

This is the love of God the Father. He runs, robe flapping, to us. He embraces us and lavishes us with kisses. The Father is willing to become vulnerable, willing to open himself up to humiliation so we can know we are loved and accepted as sons. He does what men are not supposed to do. He doesn't discipline his son for the way he dishonored him; he humiliates himself by running and ecstatically welcomes him back. With no guarantee that his son has learned his lesson, his father gives him back the title of son and, in so doing, opens himself up to being wounded and hurt all over again.

God doesn't take risks when he enters into relationship with us. He goes into the relationship knowing full well we will hurt him. We will sin against him. He isn't surprised by that. God doesn't try to protect himself from us. Just the opposite. He becomes vulnerable so we can be made whole. He shows us what it means to live as humans. To love as humans. Love that transforms is love that is vulnerable.

The vulnerable, open-to-wounding love of God is also seen when he sends his "one and only Son" into the world.[8] We see it again as Jesus willingly subjects himself to the authority of the Romans. All authority in heaven and earth belongs to Jesus, and yet, when the guards come to him in the garden, Jesus submits to their authority—an authority he himself gave them! He is vulnerable to their decisions. He becomes weak and willingly opens himself up to wounding.

According to the Roman understanding of masculinity, Jesus was emasculated in every way in the crucifixion. He was passive, submissive, stripped of his clothing, and whipped. He was hung on a cross—to the Roman mind, one of the most despicable ways for a person to die. And then on the cross, in excruciating pain, he cried out and put his weakness on full display of everyone watching. In the Roman mind, there was little that was manly about how Jesus died.

When we examine masculinity in light of Jesus, and particularly in light of the crucifixion, we see a masculinity that is willing to look weak, willing to be mocked, willing to be humiliated, and willing to be emasculated. This is one reason Paul said that preaching Christ crucified was "foolishness to Gentiles."[9] How could Jesus be a great man when he so clearly failed as a man according to the ideals of his day? How could he be all-powerful and yet be so clearly weak? Paul answers this way: "The foolishness of God is wiser than human wisdom, and the weakness of God is stronger than human strength."[10]

Paul helps us see that in the kingdom of God, being powerless, tender, and vulnerable is not a sign of weakness but is paradoxically a prerequisite of strength. Weakness is simply a part of being human. In the kingdom of God, weakness is the currency by which grace is exchanged. Vulnerability is the first step in the journey of transformation. As author Brené Brown puts it, "Vulnerability is the birthplace of love, belonging, joy, courage, empathy, and creativity. It is the source of hope, empathy, accountability, and authenticity. If we want greater clarity in our purpose or deeper and more meaningful spiritual lives, vulnerability is the path."[11]

To Be Human

Masculinity that is centered on imitating Jesus accepts that men are sometimes weak. It does not require men to be stoic and detached from their emotions but makes it safe for men to embrace their humanity, even if it means being weak. Real masculinity can be emotional, vulnerable, weak, and full of grace as much as it is strong, confident, and disciplined.

This is the kind of man I want to be. This is the kind of man I want to help others be. This is the kind of man I want my son to be.

As I think about being a father, I will teach my son how to be weak, just as I teach him how to be strong. At first glance, this seems like an impossible paradox. How can one be both strong and weak? But that is exactly what we see in Jesus. We see someone who was incredibly strong in his determination to accomplish the task set before him, while at the same time showing an incredible amount of vulnerability in his weakest moments.

In this manner, I will teach my son to do hard things, to have confidence in himself, and to never give up. And I will teach him to cry and to courageously share his heart when he fails. I will teach him to speak the truth when it costs him emotionally and socially, and I will teach him to mourn those costs when they come. I will teach him to submit his desires to the good of others, and I will teach him to not be ashamed of his dreams. Because this is what it means to be a man.

This is what it means to be human.

I am not interested in my son becoming a shell of a human so he can fulfill some socially constructed caricature of a man because society thinks emotions should be relegated to the realm of women. To be human is to be emotional, and, obviously, men are humans. But because our culture does not value men who are emotional, men have become emotionally ignorant rather than emotionally intelligent. If we as men want to be emotionally intelligent and emotionally present, then we have to make it acceptable for our men to experience moments of weakness and vulnerability. Because they will have those moments. All of us will. No one gets through life unscathed by the brutality of a world that is not as it should be. Weakness and vulnerability are, in fact, the very human act of courageously admitting there are things in the world we cannot fix, leaving us to do the one thing we can do: cry out for God to step in and do that which we cannot do. If we do not allow men to cry out to God with the full force of their emotions because they have to maintain some fraudulent sense of masculine strength, then we rob them of their humanness.

To teach my son all that, I need to learn and live all that.

CHAPTER 7

THE FALL OF A MAN

Failure isn't fatal, but failure to change might be.

John Wooden

Mountain climbers know that the most important part of the journey is the descent. The climb provides the adrenaline rush. Everyone looks forward to the climb, because standing on the top of the world, smiling for pictures after conquering the mountain, brings the glory.

Ascending makes you feel like a hero. Descending keeps you alive.

Ascent is the way of the world. Climb the corporate ladder. Get the bigger house. Increase your portfolio. Gain prestige and recognition. Build the Tower of Babel so we can reach the heavens on our own. Men are accustomed to this world. Climb, climb, climb. Ascending in the world is the way in which men prove themselves. But the world doesn't just need men who stand on the tops of mountains; it needs men who have been in the valleys and understand the important, life-saving reasons to pay attention to and value the descent.

Something profound happens when we come face-to-face with the limitations of our abilities, the vainness of our dreams, or the consequences of our sin. These experiences lay bare everything we have been trying to hide or prove. We are left naked, exposed, in need of grace. Descent is a form of death, a stripping away of all that is not true to the man God intends us to be. There, in that vulnerable place, in the valley, we find grace.

And we find we are enough.

This is the journey of descent.

The idea of descent is all over the Bible. Most obvious is Jesus' descent into the grave, but we can add Jonah's into the huge fish, Job's into misery, Saul's into blindness, David's into adultery, King

Saul's into fear, Adam and Eve's from the garden, and on and on. Often painful, these experiences of descent are some of the most important formational moments in the lives of men and women. Our willingness to descend will determine whether the journey shapes us into a bitter person or into a person keenly aware of their humble dependence on Christ. The key, then, is not to try to avoid descending into the valleys of life, but to see these descents as essential to the human experience, trusting that even though we walk through the darkest valleys, we will not fear any evil, for our Lord, the great Shepherd, is with us.[1]

A Story of Ascent

Titles used to be important to me. Not just titles, but any position that caused people to take notice of me. The title, position, or award necessitated a recognition of my uniqueness and affirmed what I felt about myself: I am somebody. My aspirations for becoming a doctor were likely motivated by this desire—and by money.

During high school I was convinced I was going to be in the medical field, but I wasn't always sure I wanted to be a doctor. In fact, I started my college career thinking I would pursue physical therapy. As a freshman, I job-shadowed a physical therapist for a couple of months. One day while I was waiting for a patient to arrive, I began thumbing through a list of jobs in the hospital network connected to the therapist's office. For the first time, I saw what physical therapists made. It didn't take long to do the math and determine that, for two more years of school, I could become a doctor and make a lot more money. Within a year, I was majoring in chemistry and had transferred schools.

Nothing says altruism like money.

Technically, I was in college to prepare me to go to medical school. Most of the other premed students in my classes studied a lot. Not me. I spent the majority of my time volunteering and eventually working as a student staffer with Young Life. I loved Young Life. Despite the fact that I grew up in the church, it was through Young Life that faith in Jesus became personal for me. Everything about the ministry brought me joy—the emphasis on relationships, the way it didn't take itself too seriously, hanging out with high school students, summer camps—everything. So while my premed peers were studying, I was hanging out in lunchrooms, playing Frisbee golf, going to soccer games, and taking high school students out to lunch.

Not really how people get into medical school.

One night, I was sitting in the Kletz, a café on Hope College's campus, with a bunch of friends. My good friend and roommate, Derek, looked at me and out of the blue said, "Pyle, you know you're going into ministry and not going to be a doctor, right?"

No, Derek, I did not.

Which is exactly what I told him. Ardently. Again and again. We actually got into a fight that night over this issue. Not a fistfight, but I was pissed at him because he would not let it go. Over and over, he kept saying, "You are not going to be a doctor; you are going to be in ministry." He was saying what I didn't want to be true. I didn't want to go on staff with Young Life. I didn't want to be in ministry. I didn't want any of that. And so I fought him and told him he couldn't be more wrong about my future.

During the summer between their junior and senior years, prospective medical school students take the MCAT and fill out medical school applications, which, even in 2001, was done online. Since I didn't have my own computer, I had to go to the library to fill out my application. At one point, I was required to list all my extracurricular activities. I filled it out: working with Young Life, leading Bible studies, going on mission trips, being heavily involved in the school chapel program. On the next page, I was supposed to list my extracurricular activities related to medicine: job-shadowing surgeon. Once.

I sat there and flipped back and forth between these two pages. Slowly, it dawned on me. I hadn't been preparing to go to medical school; I had been preparing for ministry.

I stopped filling out the application, powered down the computer, and never went back.

Eating crow is the worst. It still pains me to admit Derek was right.

At first glance, this seems like a story of descent because I had to give up my dreams of being a doctor to follow the call of God. But it isn't. It's a different title than I thought I'd have, but it's still one that garners respect in the world in which I live. Reverend. I've told the story countless times in front of groups of varying size, and I'm always greeted with smiles and accolades. It is a story of ascent. And while it changed the trajectory of my life, it didn't change me. That requires something different. A different story. A different kind of spirituality.

If the Lord Builds the House

Men, like women, are spiritual beings. On the one hand, being spiritual is as natural as breathing to us. Everyone is born with a bent toward recognizing something outside of us. Something that is greater and beyond us and yet, paradoxically, in us. Despite these natural inclinations, we still need to learn how to be spiritual in a way that takes us beyond ourselves. Without learning this, our spirituality becomes anemic, simply a tool we can wield to build the external life we dream about. Swung like a metaphysical hammer to build what we want for ourselves, it does not produce transformation leading to wholeness. It's simply self-help cloaked in spiritual language.

As men, we love to take action in the world. If there is anything that is generally true of being male, it is the desire to do something. Make something. Move something. Break something. Men tend to be action oriented. It is fair to say, as Catholic writer Richard Rohr writes, "A masculine spirituality would emphasize movement over stillness, action over theory, service to the world over religious discussions, speaking the truth over social niceties, and doing justice instead of any self-deserving 'charity.'"[2]

I love working with young adults because they are so willing to take action in the world. The world has yet to beat out of them the idealism that fuels their desire to make a difference in the world. No obstacle is too big for them, no foe unbeatable. The world is at their feet, and they are ready and willing to make a difference.

This is the "hero" we often exhort men to be. And truthfully, sometimes we need men to be the action figure hero who charges into a dangerous world. Men *should* be agents of change whose spirituality enables them to move the mountains of injustice and break the chains of oppression. "Go and do," we cheer. "Go and serve. Go and bring justice where there is none!"

It is a spirituality of ascent. Climb. Conquer. Celebrate.

What cannot be overlooked is the reality that in trying to bring about substantial change to a broken world where injustice is found in every arena of human interaction — neighborhoods, cities, nations, and the world — we will fail. Maybe not totally, but we will hit roadblocks. We will try to get to know our neighbors and have doors slammed in our faces. We will try to heal marriages in our communities and see many fall apart. We will seek to feed the hungry and never seem to have enough to go around. It isn't a matter of if we fail but when we fail.

If we are to be a people who take responsibility for the condition of the world around us, if we are to be the stewards of all creation we were called to be, then we need to learn how to fail. For this reason, a masculine spirituality must go beyond helping us accomplish something, although important. It must also change us. Often, that's a painful process. We want deep transformation to come about through ascent. Growth. Bigger and better. But often transformation comes about through descent. Pain. Humiliation. Failure. Consequences. C. S. Lewis writes about this in *Mere Christianity*:

> Imagine yourself as a living house. God comes in to rebuild that house. At first, perhaps, you can understand what He is doing. He is getting the drains right and stopping the leaks in the roof and so on: you knew that those jobs needed doing and so you are not surprised. But presently He starts knocking the house about in a way that hurts abominably and does not seem to make sense. What on earth is He up to? The explanation is that He is building quite a different house from the one you thought of—throwing out a new wing here, putting on an extra floor there, running up towers, making courtyards. You thought you were going to be made into a decent little cottage: but He is building a palace. He intends to come and live in it Himself.[3]

A change of posture must occur in us before we can experience the transformative power of the Spirit in our lives. We must abandon our ego-driven agendas. This means submitting to the will of Christ everything we want to see happen in our lives, everything we want to accomplish in the world, and everything we think needs to be done in us. We must let Jesus determine where the pipes go, where the extra floors are needed, and what walls need to come down. If we don't, spirituality becomes a pragmatic approach to the world, utilizing faith and spiritual disciplines as a means to bring about some desired goal in the world. In this regard, spirituality helps us discern our calling, like in my story earlier. Or it helps us start a ministry. Or it helps us fix a relationship. Or it helps us be a better father. All of which spirituality does do, but to truly become whole men of God, we must abandon the desire to control how it comes about and what the end will look like.

A Story of Descent

"What are you not telling me? You *must* have done something."

The words, spoken by my wife through her tears, hurt, but it was the force behind them that caused my stomach to churn. It was hard enough to stay on the road with tears in my eyes. The pain in her voice only added to the confusion I was already feeling. Both of us were grasping for anything to help us make sense of what was happening. In that moment, the only thing that made sense to her was that I must have done something. That she didn't believe me, that she might not ever believe me, brought a flood of emotion out of me. Determination to convince her I wasn't lying. Sadness. Uncertainty.

Fear.

I was scared. Everything was changing, and I seemed unable to stop it, slow it down, or even feign some modicum of control over the situation. It had all been forced on me like tomorrow. Ready or not, here it came. Fast.

That's what scared me the most about her words. Would facing tomorrow be something I had to do alone?

I had just been fired from my first ministry position, and now everything was uncertain.

If you recall the story I told at the beginning of the chapter, you will see it was clear to me I had been called to ministry. So when I was fired from my youth pastor job because of personality conflicts with the senior pastor, some complicated church politics, and, I have to be honest, my youthful arrogance, I was devastated. I had failed. Publicly. I was deeply humiliated. How could I be called to ministry and have failed so miserably?

In a culture that is oriented around success, performance, competition, and power, failure becomes sort of like the grease left in the pan after cooking up a bunch of bacon. We aren't sure if it's useful or not. If it is useful, what do we do with it? If it isn't, how do we dispose of it? Either way, as we see it slowly coagulating and turning white around the edges, we are disgusted by its presence.

No one likes to fail. Any time I've been perceived as a failure, I learned to cover over my failure with a detached bravado meant to convince others, including myself, of how much of a success I am. All of us will, at one time or another, experience failure. It's just part of being human. You will fail in relationships, fail at living up to your promises, fail at following Jesus perfectly. Everyone fails. Everyone descends.

Descent comes in various forms. Failing at your job. The falling apart of a marriage. A prodigal child who breaks the hearts of their parents. The gnawing at our soul as we lay in the quiet dark of the night, wondering to ourselves, despite all we have and everything we've done, if we are wasting our life. Descent is anything that raises the question, "Am I enough?"

After I was fired, it was so easy to ignore the wounds of that experience by blaming others. "They were intimidated by me." "I was a threat because I was young." Saying things like this made me feel better about myself and helped to cover up the humiliation I felt. I could tell myself that *I* didn't fail; I was a martyr. But in the long run, playing the victim would have never brought about healing to this pain. The truth is, I felt like a failure and was hurt deeply. And the only way I was ever going to experience healing and wholeness was to lean into the pain.

Leaning into his pain, humiliations, and failures may be the most courageous act a man can do in this day and age. It may be one of the most spiritual things we can do. Don't mask the pain. Grieve the loss and failure. With trusted friends and loved ones, vulnerably share what is going on inside you. If you can't sort out what you are feeling, find a wise soul to help you figure it out. Ask for what you need.

Failure is simply another way to say we have encountered our own powerlessness. We failed at winning the game because we were powerless against our opponent. We failed at fixing the car because we were powerless against its mechanical complexity. We failed in our job because we were powerless against the circumstances. We failed to overcome our addictions because we were powerless against their control over us. On paper, this makes sense, but in truth, most men rail against being told they are powerless. We want to believe we can control the world around us and can fix every problem we come up against. This is the lie. If we refuse to accept our powerlessness, then the cross of Christ will never make sense to us, because the cross is the ultimate symbol of powerlessness. Christ, in submission to the Father, willingly took a position of powerlessness. And yet this is utterly backward to the way the world works. It is exactly the powerlessness of death on the cross that reveals the great power of the resurrection. More simply put, a willing acceptance of our powerlessness precedes new life.

A Tale of Two Courages

Imagine a grain of wheat. You can hold the small kernel in your hand, roll it around, and even smash it, but all it will ever be is a grain of wheat. Unless it dies. If the grain of wheat dies, then it will no longer be a single grain but will produce a plant, which will lead to a harvest of wheat.

Spirituality of this kind is depicted in John 12, where Jesus predicts his death and invites his disciples to, in the spirit of his example, lose their lives. For us to follow Jesus, we must be willing to die. To put it another way, we must be willing to see ourselves as powerless so the power of Christ can rule in us. This is the way of the cross. Christ calls us to take up our cross and deny ourselves.[4] The most powerful way a man can do this is to deny his impulse to rely on himself, his abilities, his power, and his strength and admit his limitations and vulnerabilities. When men fail to do the courageous work of admitting their limits, they too often turn into either shallow men who still believe their manhood is dependent on material success or bitter men who are looking for someone to blame for their failures. They are still running on the treadmill of trying to prove themselves, hoping to gain just a little ground. Insecure men, because of their failures, will be driven by a compulsion to make themselves appear superior to those around them, bolstering their bruised egos through racism, nationalism, sexism, and countless other -isms. Even religion becomes a means of superiority over others.

The Franciscan priest Richard Rohr puts it like this:

> Young men (and often severely humiliated men) will turn every spiritual teaching, the church, the sacraments and even the gospel into another way to ascend and feel superior. Maybe that is why Jesus taught mature men, not children or youth. The "rich and young man" ... will always turn the message of discipleship into another form of personal advancement. We forget that even the concern to "go to heaven" is initially little more than disguised self-interest. "What must I do to inherit eternal life?" the rich young man asks. Jesus not only does not really answer his question (because it is the wrong question), but he just tells him to "descend" from his power position, "go away and get rid of all your possessions." Money is only the metaphor here; the real possession he has to get rid of is his ego. But he is the only personally invited would-be disciple who ever walks away from Jesus. He is too young and too comfortable.[5]

While Rohr is talking about young men, I think it is safe to say that even old men fit this description when they are unable to accept the evidence of their limitations. The Bible speaks to this truth when we look at some of Israel's great leaders. Saul's bitterness toward David consumes him until he goes insane. David commits adultery and murder when he fails to accept the limitations surrounding God's sexual ethics. For all of Solomon's wisdom, he fails to adhere to the commands of God about armies, foreign relations, marriage, and worship of other gods. Samson continues his relationship with Delilah, thinking he is strong enough to stand up to her. If, after experiencing failure and confrontations with their limitations, men continue to live under the "heroic language of winning, succeeding, triumphing over ego and obstacles," these idealized characteristics can become "disguised egocentricity, climbing at all costs, misusing power, using ideology and principles to avoid relationship."[6]

Spirituality that focuses on becoming Christlike rarely looks heroic. Often, it looks like failure. It looks like a grain of wheat falling to the ground. It looks like death. It looks like Saul becoming dependent on Ananias to lead him off the road. It looks like Peter, with tears in his eyes, finally understanding the words of Jesus as the rooster crows. It looks like David being confronted by Nathan for his adulterous relationship with Bathsheba and the murder of her husband. But in that place new life springs forth. David writes one of the most intimate and vulnerable psalms, in which he pleads with God, "Create in me a pure heart."[7] Saul becomes Paul. Peter is commissioned to feed the sheep of Jesus. Is courage necessary for this new life? Absolutely. But this is a different kind of courage than men are told they should exhibit. Churches tell men they need to courageously stand up for truth, to protect their families, to not give in to pressure to be worldly. And while this is a kind of courage men and women need, the courage to be fully human is a different courage altogether. David was courageous in one way when he picked up stones out of a riverbed and stood before Goliath. And he was courageous when he was vulnerable before God and cried out, "Have mercy on me, O God, according to your unfailing love."[8] It takes courage to admit we are powerless in the face of our circumstances. It takes courage to pray like Thomas Merton: "My Lord God, I have no idea where I am going. I do not see the road ahead of me. I cannot know for certain where it will end."[9]

A more holistic masculinity recognizes, values, and encourages men to embody both types of courage. The courage to be strong when strength is needed, and the courage to be vulnerably honest about who they are and what they can and cannot do.

This is the way of Jesus, and it is the way all people, not just men, must go when they follow in the footsteps of Jesus the Nazarene. The humility that is necessary to let God be more powerful than us, more in control than us, begins by embracing our limitations. Rather than foolishly trying to cover over weaknesses and wounds with false machismo, men learn wisdom as they lean into those weaknesses and wounds. Spirituality like that requires true courage.

Retelling Our Story

It is in the crucible of their failures that talented men and women learn their limitations. While painful, learning our limitations begins to shape us into Christlike men. Discovering the edges of our ability reveals and convinces us of our deep dependence on Christ—which is the cornerstone of being human. The myth of the self-made man is replaced by the truth of the Christ-made man. Unfortunately, this kind of wisdom and humility is often brought about through failure.

During the last year, I have been meeting with a man who recently admitted he was an alcoholic. This was an extremely courageous thing to do and was completely out of character for him. He was someone who lived by the mantra, "I can handle it." A series of events brought about by his addiction led him to the point where he could no longer say, "I'm never out of control." Instead, he had to say, "I can't control this." Admitting to his family, coworkers, and friends his inability to control this part of his life brought about new humility and new life in extremely powerful ways. The man I meet with now is not the man I met with last year.

It is difficult to see the wisdom and freedom that comes from accepting our limitations without failure. We must embrace failure because it teaches us a valuable lesson we cannot learn without it. I've heard a story about Carl Jung, the great psychologist, which I can't verify, but it's a story that illustrates this point well. Supposedly, when a friend came to Jung and enthusiastically said, "I've just been promoted!" Jung typically replied, "I'm very sorry to hear that, but if we stick together, I think we will get through it." If a friend came to him discouraged and ashamed, saying, "I've just been fired," Jung typically said, "Let's open a bottle of wine. This is wonderful news; something good will happen now."[10]

Celebrating failure seems backward. The story the world tells us is that freedom is found in power, strength, might, and success, but the way of Jesus tells us something completely different. It is in weakness that we find strength. It is in limitations that we find freedom. It is in vulnerability that we find courage. The cross of Christ completely inverts the ways of the world. This is why Paul said the cross was foolishness to the Greeks. In the Greco-Roman worldview, referring to the cross as the victory of God made no sense, because the cross was humiliation. The cross was failure. Even the disciples of Jesus had no idea about the true meaning of the cross. They didn't understand it was through the cross that God was defeating his enemies. To them, they wondered if they backed the wrong horse. It looked like their guy was a failure because the Romans defeated him by executing him on a cruel and cursed cross.

I have had to learn to tell the story of my firing. It can be either a story of failure or a story of persistence and new identity. And I got to choose what story it is going to be. The rules of the world say the story should be one of failure. But the gospel of grace says it can be about persistence, humility, and mercy.

We can believe this gospel of grace and its meaning for our life, or we can believe something else. But we *will* choose a meaning. Humans are meaning-making creatures, but we don't always get the meaning of the story right. After asking a girl on a date and being turned down, we may interpret it to mean we are undesirable, ugly, and less of a man, or maybe that women are scary. But we get to choose what it means. After all, getting turned down for a date may simply mean she had other plans.

When we think of spiritual disciplines, we often think of prayer, study, fasting, solitude, silence, and confession, but maybe we should include the discipline of discovering the more empowering meaning. I'm not talking about creating false realities or making ourselves the center of the story, but about realistically looking at the situations of our lives from a different perspective.

I became the senior pastor of our church at the ripe old age of twenty-eight. When the church leadership met, I was the youngest person in the room by far. Soon I was asked to be on an important and innovative team in our denomination. While I was honored to be asked, I was suspect of the reasons. *They probably just need to fill a demographic*, was my thought. When we had meetings, I felt awkward, and rarely spoke up because I didn't really believe I was wanted there. I was just the token young guy. That's the story I told myself.

And it was a disempowering story. The more empowering story I had to learn to tell myself is that I belong. I wasn't there to fill a demographic, but I was there because those who invited me believed I had something to offer. When I learned to tell myself that story, I began to speak up because I believed my opinion mattered. I was bolder and more confident and had more fun once I learned to tell myself the more empowering story.

To make sense of our failures, we need to begin finding the empowering meaning. It could be as simple as telling ourselves, *I didn't fail; I learned what didn't work.* Notice how different that feels? After years of reflection, I have learned to create new meaning out of the painful experience of being fired. My firing was my fault, but not only my fault. I have learned that people are simultaneously saints and sinners. That the world is good and beautiful and holy, and broken and painful and ugly. This has allowed me to give grace to myself and to those who sit across the room from me. Finding the more empowering meaning in our stories isn't meant to fill us with a false confidence, but rather, it's meant to help us move toward humble action in the world.

Falling and Learning

Spring break in high school meant skiing in Colorado. We avoided Florida as if it were ground zero of the bubonic plague and went where it was still cold so we could get in a few more days of skiing before spring unveiled the grass beneath the snow. At one point, probably in my eighth-grade year, I went the whole day without falling. I'm not sure why I thought that was an accomplishment worth announcing, but I proudly let my dad know of my feat. He smiled, winked, and said, "If you ain't falling, you ain't learning."

We understand that when you learn, you are supposed to make mistakes. We patiently sit next to our children, correcting their mistakes, as they slowly sound out syllables in their early attempts to read. We encourage them enthusiastically when they fall off their bikes. We understand that grace is necessary in the learning process. But somewhere along the line, we abandon the idea of falling as an essential part of learning to get by in the world. *It's okay for children, but not for adults*, we believe.

We need to recover the grace of falling. Descent, in whatever form it comes, isn't death. It may feel like a death, but it is actually the way to find our lives. When we abandon the need to prove ourselves, we can embark on the transformative journey downward. Otherwise, we risk becoming like the rich young ruler. He wanted to follow Jesus, and yet when Jesus asked him to descend — to give up his riches and take a different place in the world — he couldn't do it. And so he walked away. I wonder how many men have walked away sadly because they didn't feel as though they could descend? Didn't think they had the permission to fall?

The good news of the gospel is that descent doesn't change our status with God. We are still sons of God. Still united to Christ. If we are going to be transformed into the image of Christ, then we need to learn some new things about ourselves. We need to see the ugliness of our sin that needs to die. We need to understand our pain so Christ can comfort us. We need to let go of our desire to control so we might be more dependent on Christ.

My guess is that we will fall a few times along the way.

Probably means we're learning.

CHAPTER 8

YOUR NAME SHALL BE

Define yourself radically as one beloved by God. This is the true self. Every other identity is illusion.

Brennan Manning

I believe in purgatory because I went to middle school. Pillsbury Doughboy is a humiliating nickname . . . and, as you recall, it was mine. Adam and I shared a seat nearly every day on the bus ride. Adam lived a few miles from my house, and since we went to the same church, I considered him a friend. Which is one reason this event had a profound impact on me.

After class one day, I was walking across the schoolyard by myself. My schoolbag was draped over one shoulder, and my head was down. I never saw it coming. Adam ran up from behind me and tackled me into a snowbank. Hard. I know this is what boys do, and I've done it myself, but something in this wasn't playful. Something in this made me feel afraid. I felt like I was being used by Adam so he could prove himself on the playground — to show the other boys he was like them and not like me.

Deep inside, something triggered in me, and I began to fight back. But not well. Adam was one of the best wrestlers in the school and was built like an ox. We rolled in the snow for a little bit, and then he used my bag to wrap me up in myself and started yelling at me. "Don't you ever mess with me! You are just a doughboy!"

Later, I noticed that my schoolbag had a rip in it from the exchange in the snow. My mom saw it as well later that evening, and when she asked me about it, shame flushed my face. I lied about what happened. I told her I hooked it on a doorway or something. Even though I lied to her, I knew the truth, and the truth told me, *You aren't good enough. People will reject you.*

Remember, humans are meaning-making machines. We analyze events and look for patterns to help us make sense of the world. Sometimes the meaning we make negatively affects our view of ourselves. Parents get a divorce, and the child makes it mean he or she is bad and could have prevented it if only they had behaved better. God doesn't answer our prayers, and we make it mean he doesn't love us or we've done something wrong. Middle school students are mean, and we make it mean the whole school is turning on us. That's what I did.

The name caught on at school. Even my best friends started calling me Pillsbury Doughboy. And the meaning I made was more than just that my social groups were changing—they were turning against me. Or at least that is what I made it mean.

I saw that pattern everywhere, making me believe it was true.

After that day in the snowbank, I needed to prove to everyone I wasn't the Pillsbury Doughboy. But to do that, I couldn't show I was soft. So I had to hide the parts of me that were more vulnerable, kill the tender aspects of my personality, lest they come out and result in people confusing that tenderness with the anemic softness of the Pillsbury Doughboy.

A number of experiences in middle school formed the characteristics of my false self. It was there I began to believe that who I really was—tenderhearted, intelligent, disciplined, emotional, sometimes scared—wasn't enough. Middle school is where I began to dress up, every day, as someone else.

That's when I learned how to protect myself. No, I didn't take karate. I learned how to project an image that people wouldn't reject. Look good; be smart; have the right answers; don't talk about how you feel—and then people won't reject you. Don't let people get close; don't be the real you; don't be authentic—and then people will stay at an arm's length. And if you can keep people at arm's length, then you won't get hurt when they reject you ... because they will. Even those you think you can trust will eventually reject you. So never let people get too close. This is how I kept myself from getting hurt.

I was protected behind the shiny veneer of being a guy who had it all together. This guy was confident (read, cocky), high on self-esteem (arrogant), and courageous (show-offy) enough to do his own thing (lonely and trying to fit in somewhere). When I did feel rejection, the narrative in my head was often, *I'm better than they are.* This was my defense mechanism against getting hurt. And it worked. The only problem was that it also worked really well at protecting me from intimacy.

My image was built around the needs of a thirteen-year-old boy who got shoved around in a snowbank. Which meant that the majority of my decisions in life were made by a thirteen-year-old boy. Which meant that when I walked into a roomful of people who intimidated me or who I wanted to impress, I was a thirteen-year-old boy.

Years later, at the age of thirty-one, I sat down with my friend Jim in Houston. For the first time ever, I shared this story—and the legacy it had left downstream. It was the first time I had ever expressed all these things. We stood there looking at each other, both of us with tears in our eyes. He laid his hands on my shoulders, and after I told him all these things (yeah, we were there for a while) he looked me in the eyes and said two things. First, that after two years of knowing each other, he had never felt more connected than he did to me in that moment. And second, that if I would continue to grow in authenticity and vulnerability, I would stop feeling like a thirteen-year-old boy and start feeling like a man.

The first part about us feeling connected meant a lot. It made me feel safe, despite the exposure I was feeling in that moment.

The second part? I thought that was a bunch of psychobabble fluff.

But he was exactly right. Something shifted in me that day. The Doughboy was being put to death. His death didn't come about in the way I thought it would. I thought he would die when people saw how strong I was. So I hid the weak parts of me. Surprisingly, when I let the weak parts of me be seen and known, that's when the Doughboy was put to death and I could live under a new name. My name.

Nathan.

For the first time, I began to clearly see that the pain of not being vulnerable was less than the pain of not being known. This awareness was slow, like waking up in the morning and gradually becoming aware of your surroundings.

My relationships began to deepen. I worried less about what others thought of me and began to share myself with others—even when it was uncomfortable. Key to this transformation was recognizing my responsibility in being known. It's not other people's responsibility to get to know me; it is my responsibility to let them know me. People only get to see what you let them see. They will only know as much as you want them to know.

If you want to be known, it's your responsibility to make being known a possibility. Either way—from exposure or isolation—there is going to be pain. It is a fact of life you cannot get away from. Jim's grace gave me the courage to be vulnerable not just with him but increasingly over the years in all my relationships. I realized that, not only am I strong enough to be vulnerable, but I can be vulnerable and survive.

For years, I needed to prove to everyone I wasn't the Pillsbury Doughboy. In trying not to be the soft pastry man, I ignored a large part of who I was. The only way the true me—the part I ignored, hid, and even tried to kill—could be resurrected was if the false self I was allowing to live my life died.

Then I would be known.

As important as vulnerability is, it isn't the end goal. Intimacy is. With God. With family and friends. We were meant to know and be known. It is a need we work to get met in a variety of ways. We posture and politick and placate in an effort to be known without having to be vulnerable, but vulnerability and authenticity are our only hope for truly being known in a way that fosters intimacy. Being known is the catalyst for personal transformation.

Failing revealed my limitations. The courage to admit my failure and limitations is what made me a man. Something about the experience of opening myself up and letting out the real me, the one who was lonely and unknown and scared, into the world taught me that I, not the false self with its manufactured bravado and trumped-up confidence, could survive in the world. That wasn't who I was. It wasn't my true identity. It was an identity I had adopted because of the meaning I made out of experiences early in my life.

C. S. Lewis captures the transformative power of being known — even at our weakest moments — in *The Voyage of the Dawn Treader*. The adventurers, in their travels, come upon a trove of treasure arousing the worst in the boys. One of the boys, Eustace, morphs into a dragonish monster reflecting the greed of his heart. As a dragon, he meets with Aslan, the great lion of the land (although Eustace doesn't recognize him at the time). Aslan takes Eustace through an undragoning process, removing the scales from his flesh, restoring him to humanness. Later, Eustace recounts his experience to Edmund.

"I think you've seen Aslan," said Edmund.

"Aslan!" said Eustace. "I've heard that name mentioned several times since we joined the *Dawn Treader*. And I felt — I don't know what — I hated it. But I was hating everything then. And by the way, I'd like to apologize. I'm afraid I've been pretty beastly."

"That's all right," said Edmund. "Between ourselves, you haven't been as bad as I was on my first trip to Narnia. You were only an ass, but I was a traitor."

"Well, don't tell me about it, then," said Eustace. "But who is Aslan? Do you know him?"

"*Well — he knows me*," said Edmund. "He is the great Lion, the son of the Emperor-beyond-the-Sea, who saved me and saved Narnia. We've all seen him. Lucy sees him most often. And it may be Aslan's country we are sailing to."[1]

Being known. Failures, weakness, warts, and all. The best of us and the worst of us, brought before all of who God is. Intimacy. That's what transforms us.

When God Sees You

Bringing all of who we are to all of who God is. This is the beginning of finding out why God calls us beloved. Experiencing God's love for us is the beginning of finding our new identity.

Remember quiet Jacob, who preferred to hang out around the tents and cook? After the soup incident, the relationship between Jacob and Esau quickly deteriorated. As their father, Isaac, was dying, Jacob dressed himself like Esau (which included attaching fur to his arms because of how hairy his brother was, again proving Esau's masculine superiority) and tricked his father into giving him Esau's blessing. Enraged, Esau threatened to kill Jacob. Jacob fled, fearing for his life.

Sometime later, Jacob and Esau cross paths again. Jacob, fearing the worst, prepares to meet his estranged brother by dividing his possessions into a gift. A large gift. Five hundred thirty animals in all. In others words, Jacob was trying to buy his brother's grace.

Can you imagine the anxiety Jacob felt the night before meeting with Esau? Jacob had tricked their father into giving him Esau's birthright. He had stolen from his own brother. Not only that, but Esau was the wild man who loved hunting and wilderness. I have to believe Jacob was worrying about the upcoming meeting with his brother. *Will my brother forgive me? Will he try to kill me? What will I do if he attacks me? Did I give him enough animals? If he does attack me, can I defend myself?*

Am I man enough?

Sitting alone, Jacob wrestles with these questions and suddenly, out of nowhere, a strange man begins to wrestle with him. We are told nothing about this man, only that he and Jacob wrestle. All night, they roll around on the ground, trying to overpower each other, no one getting the upper hand over the other. It seems to be an even match. As the sun begins to rise, the stranger, seeing he isn't going to pin Jacob, touches the socket of Jacob's hip, wrenching the hip in such a way that for the rest of his life Jacob will walk with a limp.

And then it becomes clear to Jacob. He isn't wrestling with just a man; he is wrestling with God.

So he holds on.

Even though he was wounded, Jacob did not give up. He continued to hold on to the man, demanding that he be blessed. The tenacity Jacob displayed while wrestling with the stranger in the middle of the night is the story of his life. He held on to his brother's heel as they were exiting the womb. He tricked his father into blessing him rather than Esau. He worked fourteen years to marry the woman he loved, Rachel. Over and over again, we see Jacob struggling to get what he wants out of life. Wrestling with the world to ensure something better. And now, he is struggling and wrestling with God himself.

I wonder if Jacob saw himself as a wrestler? Could he see this thread weaving the most important moments of his life into a single garment? I wonder if it surprised him when, in the end, God blessed him? We don't know what kind of blessing Jacob was after, but I know what I would want. Security, land, prestige, money, more sons. Jacob didn't get any of that. He got a new name. A new identity.

Israel.

The one who struggles with God.

This story always bothers me because the text tells the story as if God and Jacob are fairly matched. The text reads, "When the man saw that he could not overpower him, he touched the socket of Jacob's hip ..."[2] This contradicts everything I know about God.

A man should not be able to wrestle with God to the point that God cannot overpower him. After all, we cannot even look at God without dying. There is no possible way that Jacob can go toe-to-toe with God in a wrestling match.

Unless God lets him.

My son is four, and nearly every day we get down on the floor and wrestle. Starting at the other end of the room, my son will run at me, diving to tackle me, and then we roll around on the ground. He starts on top, and then I roll over and get him on his back. He struggles and pushes, grunting and smiling, until he "pushes" me off him and I fall backward. He jumps back on me, and round and round we go. It's a fierce battle that, despite our 150-pound weight difference, is evenly matched for one simple reason.

I let it be.

Allow me to humble-brag for a moment. Because I am a fit specimen of muscle and coordination, if I wanted, I could pin my four-year-old in about .01 seconds. But I don't. I let these wrestling matches carry on because I want my son to learn to use his body and strength, and I want him to learn that he can struggle with something bigger than himself. More than that, I want him to be close to me. To wrestle with me, his father, and learn that in the midst of any conflict we might have, we can still be intimate. Maybe I'm hoping for too much in this faux wrestling with my son, but I sure hope not.

This helps me make sense of God and Jacob's wrestling match. It wasn't that God could not overpower Jacob. God wanted Jacob to learn something in the wrestling. Up until this moment, Jacob had spent his life wrestling with Esau; his father, Isaac; and Laban, his father-in-law. It's as if he had something to prove. But maybe the person he was really wrestling with was himself. Or maybe he'd been wrestling with God the whole time. Wrestling with who God made him to be. Trying to prove himself as something else—the strong one, the smart one, the one worth blessing. But instead of accomplishing that, Jacob had become a deceiver. A conniver. A trickster con artist scheming his way through life.[3]

God comes to Jacob and, through a late-night wrestling match, overcomes Jacob by giving him a new identity. Jacob could no longer use his strengths to get what he wants. The only way God is ever going to bless Jacob is if God chooses to bless him. And he does. God shows Jacob an incredible amount of grace. No longer is Jacob "the deceiver." Now he is "Israel. One who struggles with God."

It's as if God says, *Jacob, let me show you who you really are.*

I can't help but wonder how this affected Jacob's meeting with Esau the next day. During the wrestling match, God touched Jacob's hip, causing him to limp for the rest of his life. Jacob couldn't show up to the meeting with Esau and pretend to be tough. He would have limped into the place where they met, unable to defend himself and in need of Esau to show him grace. Jacob becomes a man completely and utterly dependent on grace. Rather than showing him how strong he was, the wrestling match would have shown Jacob how weak, how dependent on God's grace, he was. Grace didn't make Jacob stronger; it made him weaker. More dependent on God. His identity is wrapped up in the grace of God toward him.

If you brought all of who you are — the real you — to all of who God is, what would he say about you? What name would he give you? What would he want you to see that you are currently ignoring, missing, discarding as insignificant?

What if you could stop trying to show how strong you are, striving to create a name for yourself, and instead let God name you, become content with your vulnerability and weaknesses — your limping — and be marked by grace?

You would never be the same.

The Initiation

Jacob's wrestling with God was his initiation into a new life. Every step Jacob took reminded him that he wasn't who he used to be. Every limp reminded him of God's grace that gave him a new name. Jacob's new identity came to him through an experience that gave him the courage to be human. To be weak and vulnerable and in need.

When we think of initiation rites, we typically imagine an intense trial designed to test strength and resolve. We see an example of this kind of initiation in the Tewa people of New Mexico. These serene farmers had given up all warfare and yet, despite their peaceful existence, have a very arduous rite of passage to make their boys men. Before they are willing to declare a boy to be a man, they require the boy to go through severe hazing and testing.

Sometime between the ages of twelve and fifteen, the boys are taken from their homes by a group of men and brought to a secret location, where the boys are ritually purified as they begin their transition to manhood through an initiation. After the purification, each boy is stripped naked and whipped with a yucca whip. The whipping is so merciless that it draws blood and leaves permanent scars. To prove he is a man, the boy must stand up to the beating and prove his fortitude. If a boy fails in this, the Tewa people say his manhood is doubtful.

If the boy stands up under the whipping, the Kachina spirit that was whipping him comes over to the boy, looks him in the eyes, and says, "You are now a man ... You are made a man."

And the identity of the Kachina spirit? It is the father of the boys.[4]

There is something in this story that resonates with me. Maybe it is the father speaking these words over his son. Maybe it is the resolve in the boys to prove themselves worthy of being called a man. Maybe I relate to it because it echoes what I've been told about being a man.

As boys, we are taught, often unintentionally, to be ashamed of our wounds. That to be hurt, physically and emotionally, is something we should hide. "Shake it off." "No blood, no foul." "Don't be a crybaby." Wounds are something to be proud of only when, despite obvious injury, we keep on going as if they aren't there.

The story of Jacob teaches the opposite. Jacob can't hide his wound. Nor should he be ashamed of it. His wound is intimately part of his identity. What if, rather than initiating men by making them prove their manhood, we initiated them into accepting who they are and into believing their wounds may be a display of the grace of God?

Richard Rohr believes initiation into manhood is vitally important: "The contemporary experience of gangs, gender identity confusion, romanticization of war, aimless violence and homophobia will all grow unchecked, I predict, until boys are again mentored and formally taught by wise elders."[5]

My friend Erik's father committed suicide when Erik was young. It wasn't until after college when he began his career that Erik began to experience the pain of not growing up with a father. He didn't know how to face an adult world like an adult. Like a man. Fortunately, Erik was able to share his fears and anxieties with Brian, a man he was in a mentoring relationship with. Here are Erik's own words summarizing what he learned through this relationship:

> Being a fresh out-in-the-real-world adult, I thought making mistakes meant you were disposable. However, with each conversation, I learned that this wasn't the case. I learned that there is no such thing as perfection. I learned that the human body can only do so much. I learned that regardless of what I want, God has something more if I choose to let him lead this life.

Erik's mentor, Brian, has never been a father. He isn't married. And yet he, as Erik so wonderfully puts it, "is letting God use him to be a father to a fatherless child. He is teaching me how to be a man."

Mentors, coaches, teachers, fathers, and father figures all have the ability to initiate us into manhood. To initiate someone into manhood is simply to launch them on their journey of self-discovery. To guide them along the path, pointing out the milestones, correcting them at wrong turns, helping them understand the meaning of experiences along the way. Initiators are essential in this journey because, for most of us, we cannot see ourselves. Intimate relationships in which one is fully known are absolutely essential in this process. I don't know about you, but I don't always see myself clearly. There are times when I see myself as better than I am, and times when I see myself as worse than I am. I need people to see me and tell me what they see. I need people to guide me toward being myself. But that can only happen when I'm honest about what I'm feeling, about where I'm weak, about what I hope for. In the midst of authentic, intimate relationships, being known provides the security and courage necessary for becoming yourself.

Knowing You Belong

When I was eleven, I started working on a produce farm down the road from our house. For many kids in the neighborhood (and I use the term "neighborhood" loosely; think of houses within a three-mile radius, and you have our "neighborhood"), this was their first job. When a kid turned twelve, they called Ruth, the woman who ran the farm, and asked for an interview. She arranged to meet with you, and then more than likely she hired you. Pay was consistent. Every kid earned twenty-five cents for every year of their age, regardless of how many years they had worked for Ruth. This was when I started to understand Jesus' parable about the manager who paid all the workers a full day's wages, even if they only worked the last hour of the day.

While the pay didn't seem fair, overall, working for Ruth was a great experience. I look back fondly on those days of crawling on my knees between rows of plants, pushing a yellow bucket ahead of me as I picked beans in the field. All summer, we picked yellow beans, green beans, tomatoes, cucumbers, zucchini, corn, and jalapeños. We learned to work as we moved irrigation pipes, hoed between the plants, put down plastic, and set cages. If you worked hard, Ruth often invited you to go with her and her husband to a Wednesday or Saturday farmers market and help sell produce. Getting this invitation was like a badge of honor. We often bragged about how many times we got to go to market.

On Ruth's farm, I honed my good Dutch Protestant work ethic.

I also learned what an initiation was. Every new kid in the field had to be initiated to really belong. Ruth never sanctioned this activity. In fact, we all knew we'd get in a lot of trouble if she ever found out that initiations were a vital part of her workers' culture. So they were done in secret. We waited until she had to make a trip to the hardware store or was in the house tending to something.

Initiations usually began days in advance. Typically, it began as a call between a couple of the older kids in the field.

"Hey Doug! Has Marcus been initiated yet?"

"Nope!"

"Well, I suppose we oughta think about what we should do to initiate him."

The ideas began flying back and forth: dragging him behind a four-wheeler in the mud, running through the corn naked, standing still as the rest of us formed a firing line to fling hardened mud at him. These were the type of ideas thrown out. The newbie's eyes would get big as the intensity of the suggestions kept rising. To relieve his growing anxiety, the initiate would protest, play along, get real quiet and look down at his bucket, or try to convince himself we were joking. But we weren't.

The initiation had already begun.

The actual initiation was always less intense than the ideas. It usually got reduced to making someone eat multiple jalapeños, jump into the deepest part of the creek, or, at worst, run across a field in his underwear. That sort of thing. No one got hurt, and no one got humiliated. After the initiations, those who had been initiated knew they were one of us and had full rights as a worker of the field. As fun as it was for us to initiate people, the initiations weren't for us; they were for them. They proved to them they belonged.

Initiation rites for men secure their masculinity. Centered around difficulty, struggle, and a confrontation with the nonrational (think, fear), initiation, writes Richard Rohr, "prepares the young man to deal with life in other ways than logic, managing, controlling and problem solving."[6]

We have no such training today. Initiation rites have been relegated to fraternity house antics intended for the entertainment of those watching initiates jump through hoops. Society sees rites of passages as primitive, as barbaric rituals left over from an unenlightened time. For most, they have no place in a modern, refined, individualized society. But we must acknowledge that all men seek to have an experience that establishes them as men. They long to hear words spoken over them, freeing them from the confines of boyhood and securing them in manhood. As Rohr observes, "For the man to be born, the boy must die."[7]

This idea that a boy must die so a man can be born takes us to a central idea in the Christian faith—the idea of being reborn. When Nicodemus comes to Jesus, Jesus tells him he must be born again.[8] This idea is completely lost on Nicodemus, who cannot fathom how a man can be born twice. He even uses the comical image of putting a man back into his mother's womb. Jesus explains that this second birth is different from the first in that it is spiritual. The first is natural and biological; the second is spiritual and requires a choice and a surrender.

The question, then, is "How do we help initiate boys into manhood?"

Coming Out of the Water

One of the most puzzling scenes in Jesus' life takes place at the edge of the Jordan River. John has been out in the wilderness, calling people to repent and be baptized for the forgiveness of their sins. This is a new initiation rite John is instituting, distinct from the practice of the temple, with its animal sacrifices and tithes, whereby people are being reconciled to God. John's baptism is a critique of the sacrificial system, implying it is no longer effective for bringing about a change of heart in the people of God. John calls the people on the riverbanks to not just put animals on the table to atone for their sins but to die to themselves. He is initiating people into lives of repentance and obedience.

Jesus stands at the edge of the river and then, astoundingly, gets in the water. But why? He has no sin to atone for. There is nothing in his life to repent of. But he gets in the water, and against John's better judgment, John dips Jesus below the surface of the water. As Jesus emerges, the heavens open, the Spirit descends on him, and a voice says, "This is my Son, whom I love; with him I am well pleased."[9]

The baptism of Jesus isn't about dealing with some sin in his past; this is about doing things in their proper order.[10] This is about identity.

Jesus submitted himself to John's initiation rite, thereby affirming the legitimacy of baptism as an initiation into new life. Not only is baptism an initiation into new life, but it is an initiation into a new identity. In his baptism, the identity of Jesus is solidified: "This is my Son ... with him I am well pleased." This identity informs the ministry of Jesus. It is no mistake that the gospel accounts connect Jesus' baptism and identity as the Son of God with the immediate sending out into the world, where he is tempted to put that identity to the test in illegitimate ways.

Built into our faith is a rite of passage in which the initiate must accept their own death in the waters of baptism. All of us who were baptized into Christ Jesus were baptized into his death. We were buried with him, so with him we might be raised from the dead. Following Jesus, we submit ourselves to the waters in an act of dying to ourselves so we might emerge united to the life of Christ. Our union with Christ is where our identity is found. As the Orthodox theologian Alexander Schmemann puts it, "It is only when we give up freely, totally, unconditionally, the self-sufficiency of our life, when we put all its meaning in Christ, that the 'newness of life' is given to us."[11] Baptism is our precursor to being sent out into the world as adopted sons and ministers of reconciliation.

Inspired by baptism, I can imagine new forms of initiation rites in the community of the church that are laced with creativity and meaning. Harkening back to ancient practices, emphasis can be placed on the death of the false self—the self that finds worth apart from Christ. Or as Paul calls it, "to put off your old self."[12] As the old self goes under the water to die with Christ, our true name is spoken over us as we emerge.

I grew up in a church that practices infant baptism. Following the baptism, the pastor took the child and paraded him or her around the church, introducing the congregation to the child. Part of the introduction was telling us the child's name and its meaning. The pastor, on behalf of the congregation, would pray that the child would grow into his or her name.

Can you imagine how powerful it would be to continue a form of that practice with adults? What if we helped them live into their name? Or discover their true name? Beloved of God. Son of God. Brother of Christ. And then, as they stood in front of the congregation with the baptismal waters dripping off them, we introduced them as forgiven, washed clean, possessors of a new identity in the covenant family?

Maybe it looks something like this:

> This is Nathan. His name means "gift from God," and today we recognize that as true. We celebrate him, and we pray he will continue to bless us as we bless him. Today he stands before us as a man, loved by God, redeemed by Christ, adopted as God's son, and empowered by the Holy Spirit. There is nothing left for him to prove, for through Christ he is deemed worthy. Let us commission him for service in the world. When he fails, may he remember this water, his forgiveness. May he be secure in his sonship so he, in dying to himself, courageously and humbly serves the least of us, in whom we find Christ himself.

Baptism is our initiation into the kingdom of God. We would do well to take time to let the words wash over all of us: "In your baptism you die to your life, and you rise, united to Christ in his resurrection, as an adopted son. Jesus, the pioneer and perfecter of our faith, is not ashamed to call you brother."[13]

How many men need to hear those words? *Jesus is not ashamed to call you brother.*[14]

You are an adopted son of God.

To Those Who Have Gone Before

Understanding our initiation into the kingdom of God is not an individual endeavor. Men need to walk with other men so these truths are experienced. Knowledge does not transform; experience transforms. There is something powerful about an older man coming alongside a younger man and helping him navigate the world with confidence. Discipleship is a key way for the church to come alongside men and secure them in their masculinity. We need those who have gone before us to come around and help us see what it is we can't currently see.

The church needs mature men to mentor young men; we need men who have long ago left behind the idea that masculinity is machoism, who are courageous enough to be vulnerable, and who are rooted in their identity in Christ. The church needs mature men to take younger men under their wings and teach them, model for them, what secure masculinity looks like. The church needs mature men to be the voice that speaks over young men, giving them a new identity and reassuring them of their place in the world as men.

That's what Jim did for me. He helped me see how I was hiding and paralyzed by my fear of being vulnerable. He helped me see how my relationships were being affected and how I had areas in my life where I was habitually disobedient to Jesus. Without him, I would be doing the same thing as always. I would be just as lonely, just as inauthentic, and just as insecure in my masculinity. If we rediscover a costly, sacrificial discipleship that calls men to die and then initiates them into new life in Christ, we will see a resurgence of men in the church. Not chest-thumping, macho men, but men who are confident, vulnerable, teachable, humble, active in the world, and gentle with those around them. Men who are unafraid of conflict and resolute in their ways because they have laid down their desire to prove themselves, died to their natural inclinations, and risen united with Christ.

Men who have heard the voice spoken over them: "You are an adopted son. You are man enough."

CHAPTER 9

FULLY HUMAN

The glory of God is man fully alive.

Saint Irenaeus

After my experience at the retreat in Houston, I returned to Indianapolis with a homework assignment. Normally, this would not have bothered me because school always came fairly easy to me. Typically, homework involves finding an answer or completing some assignment where you are able to control how it makes you look. You can go above and beyond for the project and look good. You can solve a difficult problem, show your mastery of a concept, and come out looking like an all-star. For this reason, homework never bothered me. It made me look good. I like things that make me look good.

But this homework assignment was different from any other homework assignment I had done. This one had the potential to ruin the image I had worked so hard to perfect.

My assignment was to sit down with two or three people, at different times, and tell them about my experience in Houston — about what I had learned and about the impact my inauthenticity has had on my relationships.

But that wasn't the whole assignment. If that had been it, it wouldn't have been terrifying, just anxiety producing. What terrified me is that I had to ask each person this question: "What impact does my not being fully authentic have on you?"

The truth is that I had no idea how people would answer that question. It was a question I had never considered. It wasn't even something I ever cared about. I was so concerned about how I was being perceived that I never considered whether my desire to project a particular image had a negative impact on others.

That was my homework assignment: to give people an opportunity to share how my actions had impacted them. I was going to be vulnerable and expose myself to risk, not only by sharing with others what I was learning about myself, but also by giving them space to share with me something I didn't know about myself. I was going to let them tell me how our relationship affected them. Even how I hurt them. Or failed them. This was an altogether frightening endeavor.

So I called a good friend of mine, Geoff, and asked if he and I could find a time to talk. He knew I had gone to Houston on a church retreat, but he didn't know what I wanted to talk about.

We met in his office, which was in the basement of an old house that had been converted to offices for the nonprofit he ran. Because it was in the basement, his office had a low ceiling and small windows. Some rooms like this make a person feel trapped, but his office made me feel secure. Safe. So I sat on the black leather couch opposite the tiny basement windows. The couch was one that wrapped itself around you, even if you were sitting on the middle cushion. Geoff took the chair across the coffee table from me. We spent the first few minutes getting basic pleasantries out of the way, and when the butterflies had fully taken over my stomach, I started into my homework assignment. I told him about my weekend in Houston. I mentioned the growing sense of loneliness that was gnawing at me. I talked about my conversation with Jim—the questions he asked and the realization I had about how my inauthenticity and lack of vulnerability isolated me. I told him about the effect this was having on my relationship with God and the suspected effect it was having on my relationships with others.

And then I asked him the question I was dreading: "But I need to know: What is the impact of my way of being on you?"

He paused, looked me straight in the eyes, and said, "You really want to know how that impacts me?"

My heart raced. Geoff could say things succinctly. He and I had known each other for a couple of years through a pastors group that met once a month for support and prayer. So I knew that what he was about to say was going to be a laser beam to my heart, but I also trusted it would come from a place of love for me.

But I still braced myself. I hate looking bad, and I knew that, even though he loved me, I was going to feel like I looked bad.

"I need to know that," I said.

He looked at me and spoke slowly. "I always walk away from our conversations thinking about how intelligent you are, how well you carry yourself, how much you have to contribute to the world, and how well-spoken you are. But I never walk away feeling loved by you."

I sucked in a breath. It was like I had gotten punched in the gut. I looked down at my feet as those words rang in my head.

I never walk away feeling loved by you.

That was not what I expected to hear. I had always thought of myself as a caring, compassionate guy who was attentive to the needs of others. But what I had just heard was that my fear of rejection and concern for my image were hampering my ability to love others. And I was a pastor! What kind of pastor doesn't love well?

I took a deep breath, looked up at Geoff, and with as much sincerity as I've ever said anything, said, "I'm so sorry. I never knew."

My old self would have retreated from this conversation, seeing Geoff's response as a kind of rejection. But for the first time in my life, I was able to hear this, not as a rejection of me as a person, but as an acknowledgment of my brokenness. I have long learned the party line of, "I am a sinner," but this was the first time I saw my sin and how it has broken me.

This was something altogether different from learning to follow all the rules to make sure I was avoiding sin. For the first time, I was seeing how I impact the world around me in both positive and negative ways. I wasn't sitting on that couch because I wanted to be more moral; I was there because I wanted to be whole. The problem with judging our sinfulness on whether or not we adhere to a particular moral code is that our adherence to a moral code doesn't automatically make us whole. You can avoid every major sin by white-knuckling your behavior into submission and still not be whole. You can create a laundry list of good things to do, checking them off on your way to moral perfection, and still not be whole.

This is the problem with the Christian ideal of masculinity presented for so long. Men are told that if they want to be a man, they should adhere to some unwritten "man code." Get a good job, marry a woman and call her smoking hot, confidently lead, be responsible, be a stand-up citizen, and go to church. Status as a man is based on your ability to complete the tasks. It has no interest in whether you are becoming more whole, more human.

Being a man isn't about being manlier; it is about being a man who is becoming fully human.

Moving toward Wholeness

This idea of being fully human has changed how I think about sin, the gospel, and Jesus. Most of us think of the gospel, as Dallas Willard described it, as sin management.[1] Simply put, sin management focuses only on the truth that Jesus came to die on the cross and save me from my sins. He takes care of my sins so I can live eternally with God. But this is not the whole gospel—only part of it. Sin management does not address the "good news" of the gospel, which is that we are now in right relationship to God, which leads to wholeness. Sin management does not bring about the shalom of God. It does not reveal us as citizens of the kingdom of God. Its sole concern is making sure our sin is taken care of. This is an extreme reduction of the gospel that must be corrected. When we correct it, we can begin to see how it offers men so much more than traditional masculine ideals have in the past. Rather than calling us to hide parts of who we are to conform to a dominant cultural idea, the gospel offers us the opportunity to realize our true identity in Christ and be more wholly human.

As theologian J. Todd Billings writes, "Salvation is not self-centered but is a renewal and restoration of the self precisely through orienting the self toward God, toward the church as the body of Christ, and toward neighbor."[2] Salvation gives us our identity, which shapes our thoughts about masculinity. Union with Christ does not abolish who we are, but it restores us to our true identity. In Christ, we are offered the opportunity to be wholly and completely human.

In the beginning, God created the heavens and the earth. Sun and moon, oak trees and raspberry bushes, alligators and giraffes—all creation owes its existence to the God who spoke them into being. And when God created, he created not only the physical things of the universe but also the design of their interaction. There is a design to the universe and to the way the universe is to operate.[3]

There is a design for how humans and animals relate to one another. There is a design for how humans relate to fellow humans. There is a design for how humans are to relate to God. There is a design for families, communities, work, sex, ecosystems, and everything else in the created order. There is a design for being human.

Sin breaks the design so things no longer function according to design.

Our communities don't function the way they are meant to function because the design is broken. Species go extinct from the overpopulation of another species because the design is broken. Humanity negatively impacts the environment because the design is broken. Relationships are riddled with conflict because the design is broken.

Let's make this personal. I have a design, and my design is broken by sin. As you can see, this isn't just about my morality; it's about how I function and live in the world. Learning to be human is learning to live into the design God intended for humanity—for me.

This helps me make sense of one of Jesus' most difficult commands: "Be perfect, therefore, as your heavenly Father is perfect."[4] Whenever I've read that verse, I've felt intimidated by it. *Be perfect? Surely Jesus knows we can't be perfect, and yet he commands us to do just that. What in the world is he doing? Did Jesus give us this command to raise the proverbial bar in hopes that we would be better people while attempting to be perfect? Was he commanding us to be perfect so we would realize we can't be perfect and therefore see our need for grace?* Maybe, but we have to take this verse in context, and on both sides of this command are the commands to love our enemies and to give to the needy. These are not hypothetical commands meant to teach us about our great need for forgiveness but actual commands about how we are to live in the world. Which means the command to be perfect is something we are to strive to fulfill.

But perfection is paralyzing. The moment I realize I need to be perfect is the moment I throw my hands in the air in frustration. When I cannot do things well, let's just say I don't handle it with a lot of grace. My parents have a picture (kept for the sole purpose of tormenting me) of me lying on the ground throwing a tantrum because I couldn't play a piece on the piano and was sick of practicing it. I think I was eleven. So when Jesus says I must be perfect, I do not hear that as a call to carry an easy yoke or a light burden. It is an anxiety-producing, nerve-racking, unattainable state of being.

Maybe there is another way to think of perfection.

The Greek word behind the word *perfect* is the word *telios*. *Telios* means "whole" or "complete." So another way to read this verse is to read it as, "Be whole, therefore, as your heavenly Father is whole." Be whole. Complete.

Be whole in your relationships.

Be whole in your relationship to yourself.

Be whole in your ability to think and feel.

Be whole in your humanity.

Be whole in your love of others.
Be whole in your love of God.

That's what I want. I want to be whole. Perfection and whole-ness are not the same thing. In fact, perfection can be the greatest obstacle to wholeness. Perfection is the vain pursuit of something that is not ours to attain. Perfection is a category for God alone. A perfect person has no need for God, no need for grace. But a whole person does. A whole person understands that their imperfections are forgiven through the great depths of God's perfect grace. That we need God's grace for our lives to be whole is not a point of despair but a reason to rejoice. His grace is enough. Declares me enough.

Suddenly the words of Jesus are not a burdensome yoke but an invitation to something beautiful and hopeful and attractive. His message is a clarion call for men and women to embrace the total human experience and live into the design. The invitation isn't about men becoming manlier, nor is it about women becoming more wom-anly; rather, Jesus is calling men and women to become more wholly human. Both men and women are called to imitate Christ and become like him. In Christ, we do not see the distinctions between men and women emphasized; rather, gender takes second place to imitating Christ. Both men and women are united with Christ and called to walk in Christ's footsteps. This is why Paul writes that there is no lon-ger male or female in Christ.[5] He isn't abolishing gender distinctions. He is simply pointing out that as both men and women are sanctified in Christ, they begin to exhibit similar Christlike characteristics.

Richard Rohr puts it like this: "The category of human is deeper than any cultural definitions of male or female gender. The category of pure holiness is broader than any male or female examples of the same; in fact, they start looking very similar toward the end."[6]

The path to living a fully human life begins with an honest examination of one's brokenness — those places where one is outside of the design. This may mean we need to admit that our idea of what it means to be a man does not align with the design. Portraying men as strong, cool, unemotional, successful, athletic, courageous, skilled in leadership, and competent in being master of their homes may be the ideal we are most familiar with, but it may not be the ideal that best aligns with God's design.

What we see in Jesus is not a prescription for masculinity but for being human — regardless of gender. And perhaps that's the point. Masculinity is about being a man who is fully human as Jesus is fully human. It is not about measuring up to particular cultural ideals or fulfilling certain specific roles. It is about being human.

We often get this wrong. We make being a man or a woman about what we do. *Do you work or are you a stay-at-home dad? Do you keep the house and watch the kids or do you get a job?* It doesn't matter what we do, because what we do doesn't define us. That's the core of the gospel! And yet, when we tie role or work or duty or obligation to a person because of their gender, we are defining a person, not by the gospel, but by whether or not they fulfill those predetermined roles. But the goal of Christianity isn't to ensure that all men provide financially for their families; it is that all men are sanctified by the Holy Spirit to be more and more conformed into the image of Jesus. In the same way, the goal of Christianity is not to convince all women to be stay-at-home moms but to see them transformed into the image of Jesus. Using the gospel to reinforce gender roles and ideals redirects our attention away from its central goal: that men and women will become like Jesus. This redirection away from our calling to imitate Christ is so subtle that we hardly notice it.

My friend Aaron is a chaplain at a Christian college. He has spent a lot of time and energy discipling young men, preparing them for life after college. Part of that discipling process includes a study of what it means to be a man. Over the course of a few weeks, they examine what they learned about manhood, where they learned it, and what the Bible has to say about it. In one of the exercises, they look at the fruit of the Spirit: "love, joy, peace, forbearance, kindness, goodness, faithfulness, gentleness and self-control."[7]

Aaron then asks the students to take a piece of paper and divide it into two columns—one labeled "Feminine" and the other "Masculine." He asks the young men to think about each aspect and evaluate whether it is a characteristic more associated with femininity or masculinity. Once they've decided, they write it in the respective column. Take a minute to do that yourself.

Fruit of the Spirit	Feminine	Masculine
Love		
Joy		
Peace		
Forbearance		
Kindness		
Goodness		
Faithfulness		
Gentleness (Be honest!)		
Self-Control		

These are characteristics that all Christians are to embody, regardless of gender. And yet, in all honesty, most of them have a feminine feel to them. Self-control feels masculine because men have been taught that if they are to be competitive and successful in the world, they need self-control. Faithfulness can be seen as masculine because the church has taught us that good men are faithful to their wives and family. But kindness? Joy? Goodness? Gentleness? Are these masculine?

The fruit of the Spirit includes the characteristics God intends all his people, both male and female, to embody. That some of these characteristics seem more feminine and some more masculine reveals how gender stereotypes often drive our understanding of what it means to be a man or a woman. Often, masculinity is character-ized by power, control, and dominance. These are in direct con-tradiction with the fruit of the Spirit and with Jesus' teaching that "whoever wants to become great among you must be your servant."[8] Unchecked, relying on gender stereotypes to inform our ideas of masculine and feminine characteristics hinders the work of the Holy Spirit in bringing about transformation in our lives.

Drew was a gifted athlete who excelled in both football and basketball and garnered a lot of attention because of his ability. But he also had a temper. Always feeling the need to be the man on top, he challenged authority all around him. Coaches, teachers, and adults in authority all experienced him to be defiant and unwilling to submit to authority. Drew was not going to let anyone get the upper hand in the relationship, even if it was appropriate, and he was ready to do battle with anyone who may have tried. When his peers challenged him, it often resulted in violence. One time, a student made fun of Drew's new cargo pants, and before he started his next sentence, the student was on his back, with Drew sitting on his chest and driving his knee into the boy's thigh. If you were to meet Drew today, you would never guess this is who he was. He is teachable, a wonderful father, and humble in his demeanor. He still questions and challenges people, but now it is to help himself and others grow. He is, quite literally, a different person. This type of transformation is possible when we abandon stereotypes, making room for the fruit of the Spirit to be evident in our lives.

When the church becomes overly concerned with accentuating the differences between men and women, devoting considerable time and energy to teaching "biblical manhood and womanhood," it often finds itself drawing distinctions that are not biblical. The Bible spends very little time saying, "This is what a man does" and "This is what a woman does"; rather, it focuses on saying, "This is what a follower of Christ does."

Of Men and Women

A couple of weeks ago, I was playing with my son in the basement. We were building Lego towers as high as we could. But that wasn't the game. The game was creating the tower so he could knock it down. That's what he likes to do. Break things. Last week, we went for a walk in the woods. In the swampier parts of the woods, where standing water surrounds the trees, a thin layer of ice reflected the sun. Rather than enjoying the sun bouncing off the ice, my son tried to break as much of the ice as possible while I continually warned him about falling into the icy water.

When I play with my young nieces, we never play this game; rather, we play house. The imaginative games are always relational in nature. Tea parties, acting out *Frozen*, or having a meal together. They are always face-to-face and involve a lot of talking.

While extremely simplistic, these examples highlight a general difference between men and women. Men love to be agents of change in the world. Whether it means making something, refashioning something, moving something, fixing something, or destroying a Lego tower, we want to impact the world around us. Because this is what we want, we value those things that allow us to impact the world to a greater degree. Men revere speed, strength, agility, and power because we believe they represent the greatest potential to effect change and influence the world.

It is important to note there are exceptions to this rule. Not all men revere strength and speed and power. Some stand in awe of the ability to create — art, music, poetry. Others admire the ability to imagine. Or to philosophize. Even in these differences there is commonality — changing and influencing the world according to our will.

Richard Rohr outlines the differences he sees in women: "This agentic quality is in counterpoint to the relational preference of most women. Yes, there are plenty of exceptions, but it is no surprise that women prefer circles of sharing to pyramids and hierarchies. They prefer conversation to construction. They will usually choose nurturance and empathy over competition and climbing. They will normally choose connection over simple performance games."[9]

The danger is to read these differences between men and women, or any differences, and entrench ourselves deeper into gender distinctions because "that's just the way we are."

Did Jesus come to make men more masculine and women more feminine? Of course not. That wasn't part of his message at all. Jesus came to reconcile us to God and to each other. He came to free us from our sins and model for us what it means to live a fully human life.

Jesus embodied both masculine and feminine characteristics. If masculinity has an agentic quality to it, no one is more masculine than Jesus. After all, he created all there is. Go ahead, try to compete with that. Or, how about Jesus' ability to bring about change in people's understanding of the kingdom of God? Or physical change by healing a man born blind? That said, notice how different this Jesus is compared to the hypermasculine warrior Jesus promoted by so many. Jesus' masculinity was found, not in his willingness to get in a fight, but in his persistent efforts to bring about change and wholeness in the world.

What makes Jesus so deeply human is seen also in the ways he embodied feminine characteristics. Jesus worked for change not simply by being a hard-nosed defender of truth but also by being a nurturer of relationships.

- To a tax collector, Jesus said, "Zacchaeus, I'm going to stop everything I'm doing to go to your house and have a meal with you."[10]
- In an impassioned address to the religious leaders, Jesus said, "I wish I could gather the entire city to myself like a mother hen does with her chicks."[11]

- To his overly protective disciples, Jesus said, "Let the little children come to me. Don't push them aside, and don't think I'm too important for them. I want to spend time with them."[12]

And don't forget how he changed our thoughts of hierarchy, position, and competition.

- To his overly ambitious disciples, Jesus said, "Don't fight over position and who sits to the right or to the left. The first shall be last, and the last shall be first."[13]
- To a befuddled Peter, Jesus said, "Unless I get on my knees and wash your feet, you will not be clean."[14]

Jesus showed us that to be fully human is to embrace the masculine and feminine qualities that exist within all of us. The path to wholeness begins by walking the road marked for you. If you like to cook, then cook. Write a poem. Tuck your kids in at night, and sing the songs. Learn to paint. Cry during movies. Be weak. As men, if we want to be fully human, we can no longer fear the feminine qualities that make us human. Living in fear of being perceived as feminine short-circuits any pursuit of wholeness we might be engaged in. If we understand that we are man enough, then we can rest assured that any display of a "feminine" characteristic does not make us less of a man.

Just look at David. He faced Goliath, led armies into battle, and stood up to a king who had lost his mind. He was a man's man. And yet he was fully connected to his emotions. He wrote some of the most deeply emotive psalms in the Bible. This wasn't *despite* him being a man, but precisely because he was a man who had learned to be fully human. Read through the psalms, and you'll find that they aren't a manifesto of manliness; rather, they are human. They are full of joy and praise, sorrow and despair, hope and comfort, and weakness and frustration. Men and women are comforted by the psalms of David because he embraced his full humanity, not because he remained stoically strong in the midst of adversity. In other words, not only is it okay for men to let others see them as human, but it is necessary and comforting.

Through the Holy Spirit, you and I are empowered to live life like Jesus. In other words, as empowered people you and I are to live fully human, fully alive lives. So for all we could say about the differences between men and women, following Jesus is not about how men and women are different but about how they become fully human.

We can conclude, then, that men and women need one another. I need women in my life who remind me to set aside my ambition to succeed so I can be more present in relationships. I need them to remind me that nurturing has just as much value as building. Likewise, women need men to encourage them to take action in the world. Better yet, men would do well to remind women that they are powerful and that they can use that power to profoundly impact the world. To be fully human, we need one another.

We also have to acknowledge how the church needs both men and women to work together. If the church is overly masculine, focusing only on being agents of change, then it becomes overly competitive as it fixates on building something, and thus it disregards anything that isn't action oriented. Likewise, if the church becomes too feminine and focuses only on relationships, it runs the risk of being entirely inward focused. The church needs both men and women, working together, to help the people of God be his ministers of reconciliation in the world. The church must make space for the action, movement, building, tearing down, rescuing, defending, and initiation that men value. At the same time, the church must make space for the intimacy, nurturance, empathy, vulnerability, and caring that women value. Only when both masculine and feminine are equally valued will the church be all it is meant to be in the world.

Wholly Human

My great fear is that we are teaching our men and our boys to be half human. With impossible images of masculinity — strong, cool, unemotional, courageous, successful, mastering any and all situations, leading well, athletic, intelligent, enduring, attractive — bearing down on them, men are pressured to become half human. It denies the reality that not only do some men get emotional, have fears, not have all the answers, lack athletic ability, or need to be vulnerable, but that these are valid elements of the human experience. You cannot be human in a world that is broken and not be vulnerable. You cannot love another person deeply without opening yourself up to risk. It is impossible. We understand this, and it is the reason many men remain emotionally distant. It is why I stayed emotionally distant. I believed it was less painful to be distant from people than it was to let them get close and be hurt by them. I lived as the cool, distant, impenetrable man and found it unbearably lonely.

What I found was that I couldn't love people without being close to them.

Almost exactly a year after Geoff told me he never felt loved by me, I was driving with a friend to a church retreat we were leading. On the way, we talked about life, and in the course of the conversation, he began telling me about some of his frustrations with the church — not a local church, but the evangelical church culture he had grown up in and spent much of his life in. I had been working hard to be different with people. Geoff's words had prompted me to pay attention to the impact I was having on those around me, and I had been taking practical steps to be different. I stopped trying to look good. The voice in my head that said I had to prove myself and look smart or I'd be rejected — that voice was told to go sit in the corner. I listened more. I became curious about the person right in front of me. I abandoned loving people by coming up with the magical answer to solve their problems and instead gave them my full attention. So I asked questions. I reflected what I heard. I empathized.

I was doing all this when suddenly my friend slammed his hand on the dashboard and let out a profanity as he saw something within himself he hadn't seen before. While it was a really powerful moment for him, I was completely unaware of everything that had happened in that conversation.

Until the next day.

As I was teaching a session at the retreat, I recounted the story I told at the beginning of this chapter. I was sharing with people the pain of being told by my friend that he rarely felt loved by me. I finished the story and began to move on to my next point when my friend raised his hand from the back of the room and began to speak.

"I want to tell you all the rest of that story."

This wasn't planned, and I had no idea what he was about to say. It was my story, but I had no idea there was more to it. So I stood there, feeling like a deer in headlights, waiting to hear what the rest of *my story* was — right along with everyone else.

"On the way here, I shared some very personal things with Nate, and in that moment he loved me extremely well."

Instantly, my eyes filled with tears. I didn't realize it until that moment, but my story was changing. And more than just my story is changing; *I'm* changing. It began when I left behind the notion that I had to prove my manhood to others. The moment I let go of that need, I found I was free to be human. I began to believe that I, with my unique attitudes and aptitudes, was enough. I felt free to be who I am and not who others thought I should be (or even who I thought others thought I should be). I believe if men can free themselves from the oppressive, unattainable ideal of masculinity placed on us by culture, they can begin to be fully human.

I finished the talk, and as the retreat participants headed to a time of solitude, someone from my church—a person I had spent a lot of time with and counseled—walked by, touched me on the arm, and said, "Me too."

I can't even write this without tearing up. Not only have others felt the impact of this change within me, but I have too. I don't feel lonely any longer. I am deeply known and deeply loved by people I know and deeply love. When I tried to fit into the hegemonic ideal that our culture holds over men, I became less than human. Sure, I was complicit in my half humanness by believing the lie that men aren't supposed to be vulnerable and emotional and everything else. I've repented of that and began living whole. And in the process, I've found life is best lived when we are fully human, just as Jesus modeled for us.

What has to change in you so you can be more fully human with those around you? What posture do you need to adopt? Maybe it isn't anything you need to add to your life, but something you need to stop doing. Perhaps you are like me, putting a lot of energy into looking good and having the answers. Maybe you have a habit of "one-upping" everyone else. They tell a story, and you have a better one. How would your relationships change if you stopped?

What if we believed we were enough? What would you say differently? Maybe we would share things we previously were ashamed of. Maybe we would be quicker to tell people how much we love them. Maybe we would cry more often.

Maybe we would be more human.

CHAPTER 10

SHARING SPACE

Men are from earth, women are from earth. Deal with it.

George Carlin

I believe that all men are just overgrown boys with deep problems communicating. *Neil Gaiman*

My wife is a dancer. A beautiful dancer. When we started dating in college, she was co-leading a dance group called Sacred Dance. They choreographed dances to perform in chapel and in area churches. These weren't your typical liturgical dances, with ribbons and simple steps. The young women in the group had been dancing for most of their lives and were involved in the nationally known dance program at our college. These dancers were phenomenal.

That said, I never really paid attention to them—until I started dating my wife. Magically, I became interested in dance.

My wife currently teaches dance to young girls at a studio in town. Every spring, they have a recital, and until now, I had never been able to attend. I usually stayed home with our son while my wife was away. But this year he was old enough to go, so he and I went to a dance recital. In all honesty, it was better than I thought it would be. I really enjoyed the dances, and it was fun to see what my wife had been working on with the girls for the last four months.

The recital included a father-daughter dance. The fathers and daughters came on stage, the girls in their dance outfits and the dads in black pants and white shirts. "Cinderella" (yes, it got cheesy) played while the fathers danced with their daughters. Watching the dads try not to look at their feet while they attempted to keep up with their daughters was pretty entertaining. Yet, for all its cheesiness, it was beautiful.

The girls' faces beamed—I mean, a "grins with sparkling eyes full of love and happiness" beamed. I was proud of the dads for taking the risk to do something, for the sake of their daughters, that most of them were probably uncomfortable doing. That's the way it should be.

As I watched, I'm almost 100 percent confident that the girls were leading their dads on stage. The girls knew the steps and were helping their dads get it right. Sure, I know they had practiced together many times and the dads probably knew the steps, but the girls were leading because they were the dancers. And it struck me, *This dance is beautiful and these girls are beaming with joy, not because someone is leading them, but because someone is dancing* with *them.*

For a long time, men have been told they need a beauty to save.[1] Not only do men need a beauty to save, but, we are told, women want a knight in shining armor to rescue them. Men are knights, and women are helpless maidens. But that narrative doesn't work. Never mind the fact that as Christians we believe the only one who can save any of us is Jesus and thus men cannot be the "saviors" of women. I know few women who feel like they need to be saved. Truly. I know women who want to be loved and cherished. But I don't know any who want to be saved. All the women I know want to be danced with.

My point is this: Women want to be treated as equals. They want someone to look them in the eye, honor them, and respond to them. They want someone who sees them as a partner. They want someone they can trust and feel safe with. Essentially, they want what all humans want, namely, to be treated as equals.

The Danger of Opposites

Describing women as someone in need of being protected by a prince implies that women are unable to take care of themselves, not strong enough to take action in the world around them, and, ultimately, helpless. But that's not true at all.

Case in point—my mother.

When I was in elementary school, my mom volunteered a lot in the school. If we went on a field trip, she was there. If there was a special event at the school, she was there. If the teacher needed a parent in the classroom for something they were doing, she was there. I often felt like the psalmist David, who, as he thought about God, wrote, "Where can I flee from your presence?"[2] Everywhere I went, my mom was there. Even when she wasn't. I remember a time in high school when some of my friends started smoking weed. No one had gotten caught, but I knew they were doing it. Word about such things traveled the first information superhighway—high school hallways. How that happened without Facebook is a mystery, but it did. One day, I came home, and barely made it through the door when I got peppered with questions: "Did you know so-and-so is doing drugs? How long have you known? Are you? Because I will find out!" She was like J. Edgar Hoover with a highly sophisticated network of spies and informants planted throughout the school, keeping her abreast of all activities.

When I got to middle school, my mom thought she would volunteer at school, just like she did when I was in elementary school. However, the school didn't use volunteers much and didn't have anything for parents to do. My mom thought this was a travesty and that the school was missing out on a great opportunity for parental involvement. So she sat down with the vice principal and told her she wanted to start a parent volunteer program. The program was so successful that the school district hired my mom to create a volunteer system for the entire school district.

The school thought they were getting volunteers; I knew they were really getting spies.

I later found out that the principal had told the vice principal that her reputation and job were on the line if my mother's idea didn't work out. So we could also talk about how courage isn't just a masculine trait.

You see, my mom has never been helpless. She isn't weak and in need of someone to protect her. And that is true of nearly every woman I have met. They may not be fully aware of the strength and courage they possess. They may need someone to embolden them to be strong, confident, and vocal in the world around them, but every woman I've met has an incredible amount of strength in her. Which means our tired, old stereotypes about how men and women are different need to be replaced by more helpful distinctions between men and women. Even the fact that we refer to men and women as "opposite sexes" reveals the way we polarize our thoughts about men and women. If men and women are opposites, and men are powerful, then it follows that women are powerless. If women cry, then men do not. If men are strong, then women are weak.

Watch how this plays out.

Take the idea that women need someone to protect them because they are vulnerable in the world and unable to survive on their own. In this case, one becomes a man when he is able to protect a woman. Women, then, become a means by which a man secures his manhood. The implications are obvious. Women are objects to meet men's needs. Physical needs, status needs, or security within the male hierarchy are all needs met by women. Strong women become a threat to a man's masculinity as it challenges this worldview, eliminating the standard by which a man traditionally proves his manhood. Thus, men have long perpetuated the myth that women need protecting because it helps reinforce their masculinity.

Regardless of how one feels about the feminist movement, the reality is that feminists have done much to promote the truth that men and women are equal. Cultural beliefs surrounding the roles of men and women are changing, and this is a good thing. But it is also a point of anxiety for men. It is forcing men to find new ways to feel manly, because the old ways no longer provide the assurance of one's manhood.

As the roles of men and women shift, it is causing some men to double-down on the old stereotypes demanding that men and women conform to traditional ideals. Some resort to biology to "prove" that men and women are naturally inclined toward different roles. In some churches, the Bible and theology are used to prop up traditional roles as "God ordained." The problem in using the Bible for this purpose is the Bible itself, which has many examples of women who fulfill roles that are traditionally men's. Consider Esther the queen, who saves Israel; Deborah the judge; the women at the tomb, who were witnesses of Jesus' resurrection (women were not counted as reliable witnesses in biblical times); and Junia the apostle. Using the Bible to support traditional roles for men and women does work. Except when it doesn't.

But what if men actually believed they are man enough because of the gospel? What if that belief was changing how men lived? Would men need women to secure their masculinity? What if men and women can coexist as equals? What if men are able to be so secure in their masculinity that strong women are seen not as a threat to their manhood but as a crucial ally in the quest of both men and women to become more human? The answer to these questions can be found as we look at the relationship described in the Garden of Eden.[3] It's shalom. Harmony in our relationships. Anxiety, fear, shame, and insecurity removed from the space of men and women. There is no suspicion about the motives of the other gender. "He's just doing that to seduce her." "She's a man hater." All that goes away. Trust becomes possible because there is a belief that we are both looking out for the interests of the other. When this happens, men and women can fulfill their duty to labor together for the flourishing of creation.

The Cultural Mandate

Genesis 1 teaches that men and women were created to relate to one another in a unique way: "In the image of God he created them; male and female he created them."[4]

Both men and women have the fingerprint of God on them in their gender. Men in being men reflect something of the person of God. Women in being women reflect something different of the person of God. And together, men and women in relationship to one another reflect something altogether different about God. Nowhere are we told that one gender reflects the image of God more than another. So when it comes to being image bearers, we are equal.

After creating humankind, God blessed the man and the woman and said to them, "Be fruitful and increase in number; fill the earth and subdue it. Rule over the fish in the sea and the birds in the sky and over every living creature that moves on the ground."[5]

God instructs the man and the woman on how to live in the world in this passage, known by us as "the cultural mandate." It is where we get the idea that men and women are to steward the earth, watch over it, and, as image bearers of the Creator, care for creation as God would care for creation. Notice to whom this mandate is given—the man and the woman.

That seems straightforward, but let's think first about the mandate and then about how gender roles are often taught.

Notice there are two mandates given. One mandate is to fill the earth, and the other is to subdue the earth. One is about reproduction, and the other is about stewardship. And both mandates are given to men and women.

Both mandates.

Both men and women are called to care for creation. Both men and women are called to fill the earth. Both men and women are called to subdue it. We may recognize this with our minds, but in practice we often live as though men are to subdue the earth and women are to fill it. Churches tend to talk this way quite regularly. Men are called to work the land—to work outside the home—while women are to be caregivers and tend to the home. Biology is often used to reinforce these ideas. Men go out and work the ground, and women stay home and raise the kids, and if you don't believe the Bible instructs us in these roles, surely you can't deny that biology supports this idea just in our physical makeup.

Functionally, we separate each sex from the responsibility of both mandates. Men are not responsible to be fruitful and increase in number. That's the woman's mandate. Men are to subdue the earth and rule over it. This functional belief has contributed to the separation of spheres we talked about earlier. Men have their spheres in the world, and women have theirs, and they are separate. Social psychologist Mary Stewart Van Leeuwen, in commenting on the cultural mandate outlined in Genesis 1, writes, "It does suggest that any construction of gender relations involving an exaggerated separation of activities by sex—as happened, for example, in Western society after the Industrial Revolution—is eventually going to run into trouble because it is creationally distorted and therefore potentially unjust toward both sexes."[6]

Men and women must recognize that the cultural mandate is given by God to both genders and that we need each other to fulfill this mandate. For example, closing the gap of separation between the genders can have a profound impact on our marriages and families. Psychologist John Gottman has been tracking what makes successful marriages work and has found that when men share housework and child care, they "have better sex lives and happier marriages than others."[7] What's more, when sociologists Scott Coltrane and Michele Adams examined data from the Child Development Supplement of the Panel Study of Income Dynamics, they found these satisfying results: "When men increase their share of housework and child care, their children are happier, healthier, and do better in school. They are less likely to be diagnosed with ADHD, less likely to be put on prescription medication, and less likely to see a child psychologist for behavioral problems. They have lower rates of absenteeism and higher school achievement scores in school."[8] What's more surprising, when children do the housework *with* their fathers, "they get along better with their peers and have more friends." In other words, they learn to cooperate in partnership with others.[9]

If this describes the impact of what happens when men and women share responsibility in the home, imagine if this were happening in our churches. In our schools. In our communities. When men and women work together, the design of stewardship found in Genesis 1 and 2 is fulfilled, and creation—all of creation—benefits.

Separate Spheres

Restricting men's and women's roles in the cultural mandate has led to what sociologists refer to as "separate spheres," which we have talked about in chapter 3. The idea is that men have their sphere in the world, and women have their sphere in the world, and there is little overlap between the two. The divide between the spheres of men and women increased dramatically during the Industrial Revolution. Before the revolution, men and women had separate roles in the household, but men were still working around the house. This meant boys worked alongside their fathers, mimicking them in their jobs, their way of being, and even their dress.[10]

But the allure of economic success that came with the Industrial Revolution drew men away from the home. As men withdrew from the domestic sphere, women were forced to further specialize in it. Things that men did around the home—working with leather, gathering fuel, processing grain—could now be done elsewhere because of mechanization and newly available finances. Husbands and wives used to share responsibility of caring for children, but this ceased as children were sent out of the home for school. In turn, men spent less and less time around the house.

As a result, our ideas of workplace have begun to shift. Working in factories was hard, rough work that men had to endure. The home became the place where the man returned to soothe his weary body and mind after a long day's work. As Michael Kimmel wrote, "The workplace was masculinized, the home feminized."[11] The gendering of home and work entrenched the division of labor between men and women.

Changing roles in the home required justification, and the justification was quick in coming. The division of labor began to be seen as "natural" and "biblical." Mary Stewart Van Leeuwen writes this:

> In effect, the cultural mandate was now to be divided by gender and location: women were to specialize in being fruitful at home, while men subdued the earth elsewhere. Thus "pious women would keep their sons and husbands moral; productive men would work to become successful entrepreneurs ... and together they would forge godly homes, the epitome of Christian progress."[12]

We are seeing the impact of these cultural shifts yet today. Many still believe a strong separation of spheres is the natural order of things because of the biological and psychological differences between men and women. But what we fail to examine is how the notion of "separate spheres," which was created by men and first promoted by male writers, impacts how men approach their families and their faith.[13]

Sharing Responsibility

During our childhood, my mom always made my brother and me help out around the house. We were responsible for cleaning our rooms, cleaning the basement where we hung out, and helping with whatever chores she scheduled for us each day. I grew up vacuuming, dusting, doing dishes, and washing windows. And every time I complained, my mom responded the same way: "Your future wife will thank me."

Since then, my wife has thanked her.

My brother and I were not taught gender roles. We had as many chores inside the house as outside the house. We mowed the lawn, washed the cars, and split firewood with my dad; we washed windows, dusted, and vacuumed with my mom. We were expected to contribute to the work of the household, regardless of the type of work. There wasn't "men's work" and "women's work"; there was simply "work."

By the time we got to middle school, my mom got fed up with my brother and me complaining about what we'd have for dinner. So my mom and dad instituted a rule that as a kid I thought was cruel and as a parent I think is genius. Every Sunday, we rotated who prepared the Sunday lunch. Everyone in the family took a turn. Dad, Mom, brother, me. All of us. When it was my week to cook, I had to plan ahead so I could make sure what I needed to make lunch was in the house. I would then be responsible to cook the meal. When lunch was over, the rest of the family was responsible to clean up. Looking back, it was a brilliant move on my parents' part. My brother and I not only learned to cook, but we learned we could and should share in these responsibilities.

Dad and Mom did the finances together. They made decisions together. They worked around the house together. Responsibilities around the house were based not on gender but on who did what best. While my parents' marriage looked very traditional in some aspects, it was also very egalitarian. I was never taught that responsibilities around the house differed based on gender. I wasn't told it, and it wasn't modeled for me.

During the past fifty years, we've seen dramatic changes in how mothers and fathers spend their time. In 1965, fathers averaged two and a half hours per week on child care and four hours per week on housework. In 2011, fathers increased their time around the house, spending seven hours a week on child care and ten hours a week on housework.[14] This shift is largely the result of two things. First, families are adapting to both parents being in the workforce. With mothers spending less time at home, fathers have stepped in to help around the house. Second, men are valuing time with their family more than ever before and recognizing the value they offer as parents. Children need more than just quality time with their fathers; they also need quantity time.

These shifts have had a positive impact on the family. As we have noted before, culturally, being a man often means being as unlike women as possible. This includes avoiding anything perceived as "women's work," which can include taking care of children. But both boys and girls need their fathers to be involved in their lives, and the impact of the involved father cannot be understated. Studies have shown that having an involved father is a strong predictor of advanced verbal and math skills. Confidence is bolstered so children can be independent and have a healthy assertiveness. Girls with involved fathers are more likely to branch out into areas of mastery that have traditionally been for men only. They are less likely to relate to men through sexual femininity and are more confident in their relationships because of their fathers' involvement in their lives. Boys benefit from an involved father by feeling less anxiety about proving themselves man enough. Overly aggressive and delinquent behavior consistent with proving one is a man is curbed because their masculinity is being affirmed at home. Their ability to share roles and space with women increases because they do not fear the feminine as much.

Let's Talk about Sex

Marriage is the relationship entailing the most cooperation between men and women. It requires grace, intimacy, vulnerability, and grace. I know I included *grace* twice in this list, and if you are married, you know why I did. Within marriage we find the intimate act of sex, which is the ultimate sharing of space between a man and woman.

Christians have never thought of sex as just a physical act. It is a relational dance of intimacy between a man and a woman as the complementary nature of their gender expresses itself through an incredibly vulnerable physical act. This means sex is never just about sex. Our hopes, longings, needs, and anxieties are all mixed into this act. Which is why we are so profoundly affected by sex.

Men have a tenuous relationship with sex. Many middle-aged men will say, at one and the same time, that sex is among the most important aspects of their life and that they are disappointed in their sex life.[15] Men love sex, and yet it isn't what they hope for or even need.

In *Mere Christianity*, C. S. Lewis has us imagine a country where people flock to a theater to see a covered plate of food brought onto a stage. Once the people settle into their seats, the cover is lifted, ever so slowly, to reveal what is on the platter. As soon as the food on the platter, perhaps a steak or some bacon, is revealed, the lights go out and the people are left wanting more, as their salivary glands kick into overdrive. What would you conclude about that country? Wouldn't you think the country is full of starving people? Or at least has a perverse obsession that distorts their relationship with food?[16]

This imaginary scenario accurately describes our distorted relationship with sex.

Men tend to approach sex separate from relationship. We understand there is the relationship with a person, and then there is sex with the person. And while we assume there is some connection between the two, we aren't sure what it is exactly or how to connect them. Or men go overboard in connecting them. Many married Christian men operate as though any woman they encounter is a potential sexual partner. Countless articles have encouraged married men to avoid meeting with other women alone, to refer to their wives often in conversation, to keep their conversations short, and to limit their friendships with women to shallow conversations. While it is true that men must guard their marriages, this approach essentially says that men are controlled by their sex drives and are incapable of having relationships with women that are not sexual.

At the same time, sex confronts men with a level of intimacy that is frightening. From early on, men are told to disguise their feelings, to avoid being vulnerable, and to separate themselves from women so as not to appear too feminine. Sex, then, is problematic. What is sex if it is not full of emotions, raw vulnerability, and closeness to a woman? Men have been taught to keep what they desire most—intimacy with the feminine—at arm's length.

Is it any wonder that men engage in pornography and other nonrelational forms of sex? It's safer. It removes vulnerability and risk. Any shame one may feel about insecurity, emotions, and vulnerability can be avoided. But this leads to a vicious cycle, especially for Christian men, who know that God intends sex to be about relationship and intimacy. And so their use of pornography causes shame, which makes it even more difficult to be involved in a truly intimate relationship in which there is increased risk that their shame will be discovered.

Our broken relationship with sex is a large reason that men and women have a difficult time sharing space. If a man doesn't think he can have a relationship with a woman that is not sexual, then any time a woman comes into his space—whether it is at work, at church, or on a golf course—she is perceived as a threat to his marriage. Sadly, women are often blamed, even inadvertently, for a man being sexually tempted. Men treat women as if they are seductresses waiting to destroy our marriages. So women have to watch what they wear, how they present themselves, and what they say so as to avoid accidentally causing a man to stumble. Women become the protector of men and have to overfunction so men aren't tempted. Men are relieved of nearly all responsibility for their thoughts. Men act as though they are slaves to their biological makeup and actively believe the lie that they are not in control of their thoughts.

All of this reduces sex to a mere physical act. We may say it is more, but all of the anxiety surrounding the relationship between men and women keeps it from being more. Our emotions are too dangerous, too foreign, and too weak to be brought into the bedroom, where vulnerability is so high. But sex will only be about more than the physical act when men embrace the intimacy and vulnerability necessary for sex to be relational.

A New Way Forward

Conversations about men and women tend to focus on the differences between the genders. While there are some important distinctions that shouldn't be overlooked, we can lose the forest for the trees by focusing too much on what separates us. I believe the differences between men and women are less important than we think. Men and women uniquely share the responsibility as creatures imprinted with the image of God, share solidarity in sin, share a call to repentance and redemption, and share the grace of being sanctified into Christlikeness. What we hold in common is, for the Christian, more basic and foundational than our physical and social differences. In other words, what makes us different is less than what makes us the same.

Focusing on what is most important, namely, our commonality in Christ, allows us to find new ways of sharing space. Christian men—modeling their lives after Jesus, who displayed a new, vulnerable masculinity—will be the ones who make it safe for all men to embrace their emotions. Comfortable in our own skin, we will be able to take on tasks and roles that were previously deemed as feminine—changing diapers, cooking meals, dusting the mantel. But even more than that. Taking responsibility for understanding our children's hearts, connecting with their emotions, encouraging their creative aspirations. We will model for our children what it means to be in relationships of mutual submission. And our children will be better for it.

Distinguishing our definition of manhood from that of the culture becomes the key. A man who is dependent on Christ, who finds his identity in Christ alone, will be humble enough to do things not typically thought of as manly. Maybe this is what it means to be a people transformed, as the apostle Paul writes, by the renewing of our minds.[17] Letting go of male bravado in order to embrace servant humility requires a renewal of our minds that will transform us, as well as transforming our expectations of both men and women. No longer will a woman be seen as that "other" person a man needs to separate from, but she will be seen as a fellow image bearer of God, as someone whose presence in our lives will make us more human.

Just as our presence will help her be more human.

CHAPTER 11

BEYOND BATTLES

Manliness consists not in bluff, bravado or lordliness. It consists in daring to do the right thing and facing consequences whether it is in matters social, political or other. It consists in deeds not words.

Mahatma Gandhi

The LORD God took the man and put him in the Garden of Eden to work it and take care of it.

Genesis 2:15

Jim and I took a walk after we finished a presentation at a retreat for pastors and their leadership teams. Our presentation was on integrity, but we defined integrity in a very specific way. Too often, we focus on the moral aspect of integrity—Do you cheat on your spouse, lie, engage in questionable business practices, or swear? No? Good, you are a person of integrity. While that's one way to think about integrity, another way is to think about it with regard to how God designed you.

In 2007, the I-35 bridge that crosses the Mississippi River in Minneapolis, Minnesota, collapsed suddenly during rush hour, killing 13 people and injuring 145. The investigation revealed that the gusset plates that connect girders together in the truss system were undersized, resulting in a structural flaw leading to its collapse.[1] Or to say it another way, the bridge lacked integrity. A bridge has integrity when it does what it was designed to do. Cars, trains, or people can travel across the bridge without it collapsing. In this sense, integrity isn't about morality, but about the ability to function according to the intended design.

The Bible quickly reveals that we humans are designed to live by faith. We are not meant to be in full control of every situation, to be all-knowing, or to live merely by what we can perceive. Abraham had to walk by faith to follow God to a land he knew nothing about. Noah had to walk by faith to build a boat in the desert with no rain clouds in sight. David had to walk by faith to pick up stones out of a riverbed and place them in a sling. Peter had to walk by faith to say, "You are the Christ." This is what we were designed for.

Living by faith means we will live lives of risk. We will join God in his work of reconciliation and restoration in the world by stepping into places where we will be vulnerable. Vulnerable to failure, to looking bad, to not knowing what we are doing, to the criticism of others. You cannot step out in faith without opening yourself up to risk.

This is why the story of Abraham is so challenging. We aren't given much context to the conversation, but in the Genesis account, we're told that God came to Abraham and said, "Go from your country, your people and your father's household to the land I will show you. I will make you into a great nation, and I will bless you; I will make your name great, and you will be a blessing. I will bless those who bless you, and whoever curses you I will curse; and all peoples on earth will be blessed through you. So Abram went, as the LORD had told him."[2]

While seemingly benign to us who live in a mobile society, Abraham's act of obedience was incredibly risky. In a patriarchal society, to leave one's father's household was to leave *everything* behind. When Abraham followed God to a yet-to-be revealed destination, he left behind security, the safety of family, and even worldview, and he took up the risky life of a nomad. This is our journey as a people of faith. To a crowd of people who took pride in their Abrahamic heritage, Jesus said, "If you were Abraham's children ... then you would do what Abraham did."[3] In other words, Abraham is our model. We are to live like him, stepping out in faith into the risky unknown.

As Jim and I walked, we made small talk for a few moments, and then he asked me, "Where do you take risks?"

I thought for a moment. My heart started to race as I had a mini-panic attack. You know, that feeling when you're trying to look good in front of someone who means a lot to you. My mind worked overtime trying to come up with a good answer. Unfortunately, I couldn't think of any significant area of my life in which I was taking risks.

This was an unsettling realization because I want others to see me as a risk taker. There is something appealing about being one of those people who is willing to lay it all on the line. Who throws caution to the wind in an effort to do what they feel led to do. On top of that, I've been taught that's what men do. Real men rush into a burning building, throwing all caution aside, to save another person. Real men confidently walk up to the woman at the bar and begin a conversation. Real men risk it all and come out on the other side victorious. That was my picture of the ideal man, so that's who I wanted to be.

But I hate risk. Risk opens me up to failure. Failure makes me look bad. Looking bad, well, looks bad—and I want to look good. Therefore, I hate risk.

As much as I want to present myself as a courageous, valiant leader who readily takes risks, I couldn't come up with a single place in my life where I was taking a real risk.

"I don't really take risks," I told him. "I calculate everything out. It may look like a risk to others, but I figured out what I can do and how it will go, so nothing is really a risk."

Jim nodded as if he understood. After a pause, he spoke quietly and asked a question that cut me open.

"That's a really small way to live, isn't it?"

Risk Aversion

That question hit me square between the eyes. I had to admit that avoiding risks *is* a small way to live. For most of us, the fear surrounding risk isn't the risk itself; it is the loss and failure associated with risk that we fear the most. An economic theory called prospect theory describes this behavior. The idea is that we humans are always calculating risk and the losses associated with risk so we can make decisions that will help us minimize loss. For example, give someone a choice between a thousand dollars or a 50 percent chance of winning two thousand dollars, and most people will take the guaranteed thousand dollars. However, if we switch it up a bit and give people a choice between losing a thousand dollars immediately or a 50 percent chance of losing two thousand dollars or nothing at all, people will likely take a risk and play the odds, even if it means losing two thousand dollars because there is a chance they might not lose at all, thus avoiding a loss.[4] We naturally avoid loss when at all possible because, psychologically, a loss hurts a lot. What evokes the stronger emotion in us? Losing a hundred dollars or getting a windfall of a hundred dollars?

We aren't loss-averse just in our finances, but in the rest of our lives as well. We may not take on a project at work because the possible pain of failure is perceived to be too great for us and not worth the risk. We may not want to share our weakness with others because the prospect of rejection is not worth the joy of being known. We may not work for justice in our neighborhoods because the messiness involved isn't worth it. We do this individually and also corporately. As I have worked with churches, I have seen time and time again that the fear of change, along with the possibility of people leaving or getting mad, often stops any new venture from being considered.

Jim was right. Avoiding loss and being risk-averse *is* a small way to live. And for me, it was extremely self-centered. Here's why. I wanted to be seen as someone who took risks, so I did a cost analysis of every situation and figured out how to avoid big losses. I calculated what would make me look best, what would keep me from feeling the rejection of others, and what would improve my standing in the eyes of my peers. And if I had to take a "loss," I calculated my smallest possible loss. It was all about self-preservation. It was all about me.

There is freedom and forgiveness and healing in confessing our sins to others.[5] Yet many of us never get to experience that freedom and forgiveness because, while the gain promised to us is large, the way to get it is to take a big risk. Confess all my sins? Even *that* one? Nope, not worth it. And so we silently suffer under the weight of our secret.

Confessing my sins, or doing anything remotely resembling that, was out of the question for me. But I knew that men take risks, and so, without risking what was most important to me — my reputation — I found a risk I could take. I would willingly "stand for truth." If you want to be lauded as a man, simply take up the battle for truth. Quickly you will be embraced and celebrated as one following in the footsteps of Jesus the temple clearer, David the great warrior-king, or even the lesser known Phinehas.

Though it's a small story that doesn't get a lot of airtime on a Sunday morning, the story of Phinehas is the quintessential "stand up for truth" passage.[6] When a man took a Midianite woman as his wife immediately after Moses told the people that by doing so they would be put to death, Phinehas drove a spear through the man and the woman and stopped a plague brought about by the man's defiance.

Some would argue that in the face of increasing secularization, we should more diligently fight for truth. We need more Phinehases. We hear things like, "We need to take back culture [or win the culture wars or save America]." The terminology communicates that we are at odds with, and even at war with, culture. For many who adopt this posture, fighting for truth is really about, as James Davison Hunter writes, "the clear desire and ambition for dominance or controlling influence in American politics and culture."[7] The underlying desire — to engage culture — is a good one. But after decades of the Christian Right working intimately within conservative politics, we see little shift in the culture's movement toward secularization. This hasn't been for lack of a fight.

Maybe it's time to admit that fighting for truth isn't as effective as we first believed.

If fighting were effective, we would have probably seen Jesus fighting for truth more than he did. You have to work pretty hard to make the case that Jesus fought for truth. He spoke the truth.

He pointed people to the truth. But did he fight for truth? Sure, he cleared the temple, but that is one example out of how many stories?

Looking at all the stories of Jesus found in the Gospels, we can see that when Jesus proclaimed the truth of God's gospel of grace, he did so with words, and even more so with a faithful presence in the world as a herald of God's good news. The truth of "go now and leave your life of sin" was in the context of an act of grace toward the woman caught in adultery.[8] The gospel words spoken to Zacchaeus were uttered in his home as Jesus hung out with him and his friends.[9]

Do not hear me saying we shouldn't preach the gospel or stand up for truth. There are times we should. But this isn't our primary calling. As followers of Jesus, we need to take our cues from Jesus on how we should engage culture. And, when it came to engaging the culture around him, Jesus did it very differently from the way we do it—particularly when we look at how Jesus engaged those outside the faith. It might be fair to say that Jesus fought for truth with the Pharisees and other religious insiders. But when we look at those outside of the faith or those who had been marginalized by religion, we don't see Jesus fighting for truth with them; we simply see him embodying the truth of the gospel.

This is the good news of the incarnation. Immanuel. God with us.[10] Faithfully present in a new way as the *logos* of God, the Word, the truth of God, who "became flesh and made his dwelling among us."[11] Truth came, not as a voice from heaven, but in the flesh to be present with us. When God wanted to communicate with us and reconcile us to himself, he sent his Son to be faithfully present in the world, not to fight a battle.

Learning to be like Christ is learning to be faithfully present in the world. James Davison Hunter states that a faithful presence "calls Christians to enact the shalom of God in the circumstances in which God has placed them and to actively seek it on behalf of others."[12] The apostle Paul concludes that God "marked out [our] appointed times in history and the boundaries of [our] lands ... so that [we] would seek him and perhaps reach out for him and find him."[13] In other words, God has placed you where you are for the good of that place. God is calling you to the places you already are. Your home. Your workplace. Your gym. Your neighborhood. The Starbucks you go to. Actively seek the good of those who are in those places. Take responsibility for the kingdom of God, on earth as it is in heaven, wherever you find yourself. For my wife and me, we are actively seeking the good of the neighborhood we just moved to. We've intentionally gotten to know our neighbors. Hosted parties. Played with their kids. Raked yards so we can be agents of shalom in this place. After all, that is the way of Jesus.

From Warrior to Gardener

The idea of fighting for truth will not go away quickly. For us in America, our concepts of manliness are inseparable from the image of a warrior. Men conquer. They can conquer others, the market, ideas, and their lawns. As NPR host Andrew Schmookler points out, "Preparing to fight our enemies is always manly."[14] This is why the idea of fighting for truth is so prominent in our churches. It appeals to the ideal of masculinity that pervades our culture. Men don't have to be less manly in church. They can fight their enemies—liberal secularists, pro-choicers, Old Earth creationists, or Prius owners— you don't have to completely reject the American role of a man. You can be a warrior in the army of the Lord.

Cue the song:

I may never march in the infantry,
Ride in the cavalry,
Shoot the artillery.
I may never fly o'er the enemy,
But I'm in the Lord's army. Yes, sir!

While these lyrics may quicken the hearts of the battle-prone, I can't help but wonder if that's really what we were designed for. When God created Adam and Eve and placed them in the garden, did he create them to be in an army? Was the man designed from the beginning to be a warrior?

The opening chapter of Genesis introduces us to our calling as stewards. We were meant to care for, watch over, and cultivate the creation.[15] Now, some may quickly point out that protecting creation means we may have to fight, but I would quietly point at the text and ask: What would we be protecting creation from in Genesis 1 and 2? Before the fall in Genesis 3?

So why would we need warriors?

Could it be that our need for warriors, or even our belief that we need warriors, simply highlights that creation has lost its integrity? That it doesn't function like it is supposed to?

And if that's true, then should we celebrate warriors, or should we mourn the need for them?

Prior to the fall, creation existed in shalom. Shalom refers to a peace that permeates every facet of creation. All relationships are in harmony with one another—relationships between God and humanity, humanity and humanity, humanity and creation, and individuals with themselves. In the garden, before sin entered the world, there is integrity, with everything the way it is supposed to be—and it was very good.

The picture of the garden, that place where everything exists according to the design, is what we should focus on to give us a new portrait of what a man should be like. In this picture, we don't need a warrior; we need a good steward. The only way men will begin to embrace that role is if they believe they don't need to prove themselves because they are already man enough. You may wonder if this is necessary, but as Andrew Schmookler writes, "It is one thing for a man to guard what is his own—that is the work of the warrior.

It is another for a man to take care of what has been entrusted to him—that sounds a lot like women's work."[16] The warrior ideal is so pervasive in our culture that to abandon it for an image of a man who takes care of what is entrusted to him is equated with being a woman.

Schmookler goes on:

> For thousands of years, human communities have seen the greatest threat to their survival as coming from outside enemies. So they have made warriors their heroes, and made the virtues of the man of power their ideal of manhood ... New virtues are required of us. There is another ancient image of what a man might be. It is the image of the good steward, the man to whom the care of things can be entrusted. Until the good steward seems to us as manly as the vigilant warrior, our national security will be threatened by our very notions of what it means to be a protector.[17]

We need men to embrace their agentic nature in the world and work toward the shalom of God's creation. We need men to be protectors of the creation, where, as Mary Stewart Van Leeuwen writes, "each sphere of life is given its proper due: science, art, worship, government, commerce and family life are kept in proper balance, each to fulfill its rightful calling, with none being allowed—in either personal or corporate existence—to swallow up or marginalize the others."[18] This means we need men of every temperament to be the men God created them to be. We need the strong and the quiet, the decisive leader and the poet, the scientist and the painter—all of them encouraging the other to move toward becoming the most human man they can be.

A Final Charge

I still have a hard time taking risks. My fear of risk is wrapped up in my fear of vulnerability. The reason I didn't risk sharing my whole self with other people is that I didn't want to be vulnerable and open myself up to pain. The reason I didn't risk showing emotion is that I didn't want to be vulnerable to being called weak. The reason I didn't risk taking on projects and doing things I wasn't sure I could do is that I didn't want to be vulnerable to being called a failure. My fear of risk was rooted in my fear of being vulnerable.

And I'm still afraid. I'll probably always be terrified of taking risks. But I'm learning to be honest about that fear, and I'm finding that just being honest about my fear is giving me the strength to take responsibility in the world. It brings the fear out of the darkness and into the light so it can be exposed and lose its strength.

I'm intentionally choosing to be vulnerable. I've found it is the only way to be fully human. What's more, I believe being vulnerable is the only way to be like Jesus. And that's what the world needs. People being more like Jesus.

If we are going to be people of faith, we need to learn how to be vulnerable. We need to learn how to take risks in the world. Not the kind of risk that involves jumping out of an airplane, but the kind of risk that places us as partners in the good work of restoration that God is doing in the world.

It is risky to believe anything that runs counter to our culture. Daring to challenge the pervasive and powerful norms is risky. In many ways it will feel like death. But it is in losing our lives that we will find them. And what we find is a way of living that isn't defined by gender, where men and women inhabit separate spheres, but rather, it is a new relationship and a new way of sharing space, where men and women work together, encouraging each other to fulfill the cultural mandate given in the garden as we live into the design. As we encourage one another to live fully human lives, embracing our strengths and weaknesses, embodying the fruit of the Spirit, and imitating Christ, we begin to re-create a world that is full of integrity. Maybe not completely, but we get glimpses of this new world. Tastes of the world as it should be. Relationships restored.

Justice that flows like a river. Communities of healing and hope. Not because we picked up our swords, but because we beat them into plowshares so we can use them to steward the creation in new ways.

Taking responsibility as stewards of creation is where the risk is. This is how we embark on the journey, even though we may not know exactly where we're going. We become whole people who live into the design, and we take responsibility for the world around us. Take responsibility for your family, your neighborhood, your church, and your community. You are man enough, in Christ, to be what the world needs. Hear the God of the universe call you "son." Lay aside the anxious pursuit to prove yourself good enough, successful enough, powerful enough to be considered a man. Instead, accept the man God made you to be.

Embrace that man because, in the end, the world doesn't need a manlier man; the world needs a more human man.

ACKNOWLEDGMENTS

When I first thought of writing a book, I thought of early mornings, late nights, and coffee. Lots of coffee. Writing, in my mind, was a solitary endeavor fueled by a relentless drive of an introverted author to put words to page. What I've learned through writing my first book is that writing a book is the farthest thing from a solitary endeavor. It has been a joy to work with so many amazing people on this project. Without them, there would be no book to hold. I am grateful to and for the many who helped in so many ways.

To and for Jenni Burke, my agent. Thanks for taking a risk on a new author with a new idea. Thanks for caring about the project as much as I do. Thanks for being an advocate and friend.

To and for the great people at Zondervan. My editors, John Sloan, Carolyn McCready, and Dirk Buursma—thank you for believing in this project and giving so much attention to it throughout the process. Your work made this book so much better.

To and for blog readers and friends on the interwebs. In this day and age, your reading and interactions are a big part of the reason this book was even considered by a publisher. Thank you.

To and for the amazing congregation of Christ's Community Church. I still shake my head at the thought of you hiring a twenty-eight-year-old me as your pastor. Thank you for the privilege of walking alongside your lives. Thank you for making space for and supporting this part of my calling.

To and for friends who became early champions of this project—Nish Weiseth, Rachel Held Evans, Matthew Paul Turner, Sarah Bessey, Benjamin L. Corey, and Micah J. Murray. To and for those friends who helped me process ideas and gave feedback on early drafts of chapters. The early input of Chad Schuitema, Drew Poppleton, Seth Haines, and Brett Duiser helped me get my mind around the project. Chuck DeGroat, thank you for your initial feedback on the outline and chapter ideas. We barely knew each other, and you risked a lot by giving some critical feedback that changed the entire direction of the book. Joshua Ryan Butler, you have an amazing ability to write and synthesize ideas. I'm so grateful for your many edits and thoughts and for your friendship.

To and for Jim Herrington. Mentor, coach, and friend. You've impacted me in more ways than I can count. This book would not exist without you challenging me to go against all my instincts and be more vulnerable. Thank you.

To and for my parents. For being there, for encouraging me, and for being my biggest supporters.

To and for Luke. I couldn't ask for a better son. As you say, "We'll always be buddies." Thank you for continually teaching me how to be a man who sees the world as a child.

To and for my wife, Sarah. You never hesitated when I brought up the idea of writing a book. You edited my papers in seminary. You knew my writing long before anyone else. You, more than anyone, knew what a task it would be for me to write this book. Thank you for believing in me. For making time for me to write. When I needed to process an idea, you listened. Thank you for helping me balance life when it got crazy because I took on more than I should have. Thank you for partnering with me. Thank you for always saying yes to us.

To and for Jesus, who is transforming everything about me from one degree to another that I might become more fully human.

NOTES

Chapter 1: Out of the Wilderness

1. 1 Timothy 4:12.
2. Jason Parham, "How Should We Define Masculinity? A Q&A with Charles Blow," *Gawker Review of Books*, http://review.gawker.com /how-should-we-define-masculinity-a-q-a-with-charles-bl-1643322292 (accessed January 20, 2015).
3. Genesis 25:27.
4. Romans 9:11, 13.
5. Romans 12:2.

Chapter 2: Man Made

1. See *Merriam-Webster Online*, s.v. "emasculate," www.merriam-webster .com/dictionary/emasculate (accessed January 22, 2015).
2. David D. Gilmore, *Manhood in the Making: Cultural Concepts of Masculinity* (New Haven, CT: Yale University Press, 1990), 1.
3. Ibid., 17.
4. John Steinbeck, *Of Mice and Men* (New York: Penguin, 1993), 77.
5. Erving Goffman, *Stigma: Notes on the Management of Spoiled Identity* (Englewood Cliffs, NJ: Prentice Hall, 1963), 128.
6. See Exodus 20:13, 17.
7. See 1 Samuel 13:14; Acts 13:22.
8. See Luke 22:33–34.
9. John 21:15–20.
10. Acts 9:1.
11. Acts 9:2.
12. Hebrews 2:11.
13. Ephesians 2:10.
14. Luke 13:24–25.
15. John 1:16 ESV.

Chapter 3: Shifting Sands

1. "Pink or Blue?" *Infants' Department*, June 1918.
2. See Michael Kimmel, *Manhood in America* (New York: Free Press, 1996), 15.
3. 1 Timothy 5:3–8.
4. John Calvin, *Commentary on Timothy, Titus, Philemon*, www.ccel.org /ccel/calvin/calcom43.iii.vii.ii.html (accessed January 23, 2015).
5. Matthew 8:20.
6. Luke 8:3.
7. John 19:26–27.
8. Charles Sellers, *The Market Revolution: Jacksonian America, 1815-1846* (New York: Oxford University Press, 1992), 246.
9. See Kimmel, *Manhood in America,* 32.
10. Henry David Thoreau, *Walden* (New York: Signet, 1960), 10.
11. Kimmel, *Manhood in America,* 32.
12. William Rorabaugh, *The Alcoholic Republic* (New York: Oxford University Press, 1979), 29.
13. Edward Emerson Bourne, *The History of Wells and Kennebunk from the Earliest Settlement of the Year 1820* (Portland, OR: Thurston, 1875), 413.
14. Alexis de Tocqueville, *Democracy in America*, trans. George Lawrence (1840: repr., New York: HarperCollins, 1988), 601.
15. Ibid., 592.
16. Ephesians 6:4.
17. Genesis 29:9.
18. Ruth 2:2–3.
19. Proverbs 31:16, 18, 24.
20. Margaret Mead, *And Keep Your Powder Dry* (New York: Morrow, 1942), 68–69.

Chapter 4: Muscular Christianity

1. Quoted in Ann Douglas, *The Feminization of American Culture* (New York: Knopf, 1977), 101.
2. Pew Research Religion and Public Life Project, "Religious Landscape Survey: Portraits: Demographics," http://religions.pewforum.org /portraits (accessed January 26, 2015).

3. For current demographics of the church, see U.S. Congregational Life Survey, "Key Findings: Who Worships in the U.S.," www.uscongregations.org/blog/2014/02/17/key-findings-who-worships -in-the-u-s/ (accessed January 26, 2015). For demographic studies of the early church, see Rodney Stark, *The Rise of Christianity: How the Obscure, Marginal Jesus Movement Became the Dominant Religious Force in the Western World in a Few Centuries* (San Francisco: HarperSanFrancisco, 1997), 95–128.

4. Quoted in Michael Kimmel, *Manhood in America* (New York: Free Press, 1996), 131.

5. Thomas Hughes, *Tom Brown at Oxford* (London: Macmillan, 1891), 99.

6. Hiram Wesley Evans, Georgia Imperial Wizard of the Ku Klux Klan, quoted in Kimmel, *Manhood in America*, 118.

7. Mark Driscoll, quoted in Molly Worthen, "Who Would Jesus Smack Down?" *New York Times Magazine,* January 11, 2009, www.nytimes .com/2009/01/11/magazine/11punk-t.html?pagewanted=all (accessed January 25, 2015).

8. *Fight Club*, screenplay by Jim Uhls, based on the novel by Chuck Palahniuk, www.angelfire.com/vamp/firestarter2k/FightClub /fightclubfinal.html (accessed January 27, 2015).

9. "12 Things You Didn't Know about *Fight Club*," *Imgur*, http://imgur .com/gallery/PNPOi (accessed January 27, 2015).

10. Brandon O'Brien, "A Jesus for Real Men," *Christianity Today,* April 18, 2009, www.christianitytoday.com/ct/2008/april/27.48.html (accessed January 27, 2015).

11. Matthew 5:9, 39, 44.

12. Sara Butler, "Sex or Gender?" *First Things* 154 (June/July 2005): 43–46, www.firstthings.com/article/2005/06/sex-or-gender (accessed January 27, 2015).

13. Galatians 5:24.

14. Romans 12:10 ESV.

Chapter 5: Jesus

1. 2 Corinthians 5:21.

2. C. S. Lewis, *Mere Christianity* (1943; repr., New York: Macmillan, 1960), 161.

3. The ESV uses the phrase "be imitators" instead of "follow my example."

4. Lewis, *Mere Christianity*, 161–62.

5. Christian Smith and Melinda Lundquist Denton, *Soul Searching: The Religious and Spiritual Lives of American Teenagers* (New York: Oxford University Press, 2005), 162.

6. Matthew 16:24–25.

7. Matthew 11:30.

8. See Colossians 1:15–20.

9. Luke 22:19–24; John 13:4–5.

10. Philippians 2:6–7.

11. See Colleen M. Conway, *Behold the Man: Jesus and Greco-Roman Masculinity* (New York: Oxford University Press, 2008), 160.

12. Revelation 19:12.

13. Romans 8:17.

14. Mark Driscoll, quoted in "From the Mag: 7 Big Questions," *Relevant*, www.relevantmagazine.com/god/church/features/1344-from-the-mag -7-big-questions (accessed January 27, 2015).

15. Ronald H. Preston and Anthony T. Hanson, *The Revelation of Saint John the Divine* (London: SCM, 1949), 120, emphasis mine.

16. Colossians 1:21.

17. Revelation 5:2.

18. Revelation 5:6.

19. See Andy Alexis-Baker, "Violence, Nonviolence, and the Temple Incident in John 2:13–15," *Biblical Interpretation* 20 (2012): 73–96.

20. See Scott Lively, "Masculine Christianity," 1, www.defendthefamily. com/_docs/resources/2229290.pdf (accessed January 27, 2015).

21. See Conway, *Behold the Man*, 26.

22. Marcus Aurelius, *Meditations*, trans. Maxwell Staniforth (Baltimore: Penguin, 1964), book 2, paragraph 18.

23. John 2:15.

24. See Alexis-Baker, "Violence, Nonviolence, and the Temple Incident in John 2:13-15."

25. See Ephesians 4:26.

26. Colossians 1:15.

27. Lively, "Masculine Christianity," 2.

28. Luke 13:34.

29. Luke 19:38, 41.

Chapter 6: Delighting in Weakness

1. Brené Brown, *Daring Greatly: How the Courage to Be Vulnerable Transforms the Way We Live, Love, Parent, and Lead* (New York: Gotham, 2012), 93.
2. See the U.S. Department of Justice's "Homicide Trends in the United States, 1980-2008" (www.bjs.gov/content/pub/pdf/htus8008.pdf), which reported that, in this twenty-eight-year time period, nearly 90 percent of homicides were committed by male offenders. *Mother Jones* magazine did a study of every mass shooting in the last three decades and reports that nearly every one of them involved a male killer (Mark Follman, Gavin Aronsen, and Deanna Pan, "A Guide to Mass Shootings in America," www.motherjones.com/politics/2012/07/mass -shootings-map [accessed January 27, 2015]).
3. Dan Kindlon and Michael Thompson, *Raising Cain: Protecting the Emotional Life of Boys* (New York: Ballantine, 1999), 4.
4. Ibid., 7.
5. 2 Corinthians 12:10.
6. The parable is told in Luke 15:11–32.
7. Kenneth E. Bailey, *Poet and Peasant* and *Through Peasant Eyes* (Grand Rapids: Eerdmans, 1983), 161–206.
8. John 3:16.
9. 1 Corinthians 1:23.
10. 1 Corinthians 1:25.
11. Brown, *Daring Greatly*, 34.

Chapter 7: The Fall of a Man

1. Psalm 23:4.
2. Richard Rohr, *From Wild Man to Wise Man: Reflections on Male Spirituality* (Cincinnati, OH: Franciscan Media, 2005), 10.
3. C. S. Lewis, *Mere Christianity* (1943; repr., New York: Macmillan, 1960), 174.
4. Matthew 16:24.
5. Rohr, *From Wild Man to Wise Man*, 164.
6. Ibid., 159.
7. Psalm 51:10.
8. Psalm 51:1.

9. Thomas Merton, *Thoughts in Solitude* (New York: Farrar, Straus and Giroux, 1999), 79.
10. This story is recounted in Robert Bly, *Iron John* (1990; repr., Cambridge, MA: Da Capo, 2004), 71. I'm unsure if Bly's telling of the story is original or not.

Chapter 8: Your Name Shall Be

1. C. S. Lewis, *The Voyage of the Dawn Treader* (1952; repr., New York: HarperCollins, 1994), 110–11, emphasis mine.
2. Genesis 32:25.
3. I'm grateful to Joshua Ryan Butler for his insight on the story of Jacob wrestling with God.
4. Cited in David D. Gilmore, *Manhood in the Making: Cultural Concepts of Masculinity* (New Haven, CT: Yale University Press, 1990), 15.
5. Richard Rohr, *From Wild Man to Wise Man: Reflections on Male Spirituality* (Cincinnati, OH: Franciscan Media, 2005), 32
6. Ibid., 31.
7. Ibid., 39.
8. John 3:3.
9. Matthew 3:17.
10. See Matthew 3:15.
11. Alexander Schmemann, *For the Life of the World* (Crestwood, NY: St. Vladimir's Seminary Press, 1973), 74.
12. Ephesians 4:22.
13. See Romans 6:4–10; Galatians 3:26–27; Ephesians 1:5–6; Hebrews 12:2; 2:11.
14. See Hebrews 2:11.

Chapter 9: Fully Human

1. See Dallas Willard, *The Divine Conspiracy* (San Francisco: HarperSanFrancisco, 1998), 35–59.
2. J. Todd Billings, *Union with Christ: Reframing Theology and Ministry for the Church* (Grand Rapids: Baker Academic, 2011), 9.
3. These ideas are adapted from what I learned through Faithwalking—a discipleship process designed to help people live fully human lives on a

mission in the world (see www.faithwalking.us). It is also the sponsor of the retreat I mentioned at the beginning of the book.

4. Matthew 5:48.
5. See Galatians 3:28.
6. Richard Rohr, "Gender, God and Spirituality," *Huffington Post*, June 28, 2012, www.huffingtonpost.com/fr-richard-rohr/gender-god-and -spirituality_b_1624932.html (accessed January 27, 2015).
7. Galatians 5:22–23.
8. Mark 10:43.
9. Rohr, "Gender, God and Spirituality."
10. Luke 19:5, my paraphrase.
11. Matthew 23:37, my paraphrase.
12. Mark 10:14, my paraphrase.
13. Mark 9:35; 10:43–44, my paraphrase.
14. John 13:8, my paraphrase.

Chapter 10: Sharing Space

1. The phrase "a beauty to save" is taken from the title of a chapter in John Eldredge's *Wild at Heart: Discovering the Secret of a Man's Soul* (Nashville: Nelson, 2001).
2. Psalm 139:7.
3. See Genesis 2.
4. Genesis 1:27.
5. Genesis 1:28.
6. Mary Stewart Van Leeuwen, *My Brother's Keeper: What the Social Sciences Do (and Don't) Tell Us about Masculinity* (Downers Grove, IL: InterVarsity, 2002), 30.
7. John Gottman, *Why Marriages Succeed or Fail* (New York: Simon and Schuster, 1995), 157.
8. Quoted in Michael Kimmel, "Has a Man's World Become a Woman's Nation," in *The Shriver Report: A Woman's Nation Changes Everything*, ed. Heather Boushey and Ann O'Leary (New York: Free Press, 2009), 352.
9. Ibid.
10. See Van Leeuwen, *My Brother's Keeper*, 151.
11. Michael Kimmel, *Manhood in America* (New York: Free Press, 1996), 39.
12. Van Leeuwen, *My Brother's Keeper*, 153, quoting Gail Bederman in her 1989 article in *American Quarterly*, " 'The Women Have Had Charge of the Church Work Long Enough.' "

13. See Kimmel, *Manhood in America*, 39.
14. Kim Parker and Wendy Wang, "Modern Parenthood: Roles of Moms and Dads Converge as They Balance Work and Family," *Pew Research Center*, www.pewsocialtrends.org/2013/03/14/modern-parenthood -roles-of-moms-and-dads-converge-as-they-balance-work-and-family/5/ (accessed January 27, 2015).
15. See Van Leeuwen, *My Brother's Keeper*, 212.
16. See C. S. Lewis, *Mere Christianity* (1943; repr., New York: Macmillan, 1960), 89–90.
17. See Romans 12:1.

Chapter 11: Beyond Battles

1. Frederick J. Frommer, "NTSB: Design Errors Factor in 2007 Bridge Collapse," *USA Today*, http://usatoday30.usatoday.com/news/ world/2008-11-13-628592230_x.htm (accessed January 27, 2015).
2. Genesis 12:1–4.
3. John 8:39.
4. This example is used in Michael Frost and Alan Hirsch, *The Faith of Leap* (Grand Rapids: Baker, 2011), 135.
5. James 5:16.
6. Numbers 25.
7. James Davison Hunter, *To Change the World: The Irony, Tragedy, and Possibility of Christianity in the Late Modern World* (New York: Oxford University Press, 2010), 124.
8. John 8:2–11.
9. Luke 19:1–10.
10. See Matthew 1:23.
11. John 1:14.
12. Hunter, *To Change the World*, 278.
13. Acts 17:26–27.
14. Andrew B. Schmookler, "Manliness and Mother Earth," *Christian Science Monitor*, October 3, 1991, www.csmonitor. com/1991/1003/03191.html (accessed January 27, 2015).
15. Genesis 1:28.
16. Schmookler, "Manliness and Mother Earth."
17. Ibid.
18. Mary Stewart Van Leeuwen, *My Brother's Keeper* (Downers Grove, IL: InterVarsity, 2002), 247.

Bond of Brothers

Connecting with Other Men beyond Work, Weather, and Sports

Wes Yoder

According to Wes Yoder, a whole lot of insecurity, secrets, shame, and silence keep men from growing strong in the broken places.

Declare war on shallowness! The conversation starts here—in this groundbreaking book.

In the foreword to *Bond of Brothers*, Wm. Paul Young writes, "You want to better understand 'man'? Then begin here, in these stories and questions, these longings and desires, the explorations of risk and trust required, the examination of both profound majesty and staggering stupidity, in both the ironwork and the artistry. This is not a book of formulas and magical incantations, but an invitation into becoming, to enter the depths of disclosure that makes humans of us men, while celebrating what only we can bring to the dance. So dive in and listen for the Father's heart, the One who respects you enough to await your call, but loves you enough never to be far-off and who will always refuse to let you travel down this road alone."

Available in stores and online!